SPEARHEAD

US RANGERS
'Leading the Way'

SPEARHEAD

US RANGERS
'Leading the Way'

Ian Westwell

Ian Allan
PUBLISHING

Previous Pages: Company C, 2nd Ranger Battalion, prepares for a patrol, Ruhrberg, Germany (see page 58).

Below: Rangers training in Scotland in August 1942. The log – as taught by the British Commandos with whom they were training – forced groups of trainees to learn to work as a team, as well as building strength.

Acknowledgements
Thanks to Mark Franklin of Flatt Art for the maps; Tim Hawkins for the colour photographs; George Forty for the Pointe du Hoc photos; all other photo research was by John D. Gresham, ably assisted by Melinda K. Day. All mono photographs are from U.S. sources National Archives, U.S. Signal Corps, Fort Benning and U.S. Army with references available on request.

First published 2003

ISBN 0 7110 2978 4

© Compendium Publishing 2003

Published by Ian Allan Publishing

an imprint of Ian Allan Publishing Ltd, Hersham, Surrey KT12 4RG
Printed by Ian Allan Printing Ltd, Hersham, Surrey KT12 4RG

Code: 0308/B

British Library Cataloguing in Publication Data
A CIP catalogue record for this book is available from the British Library

Note: Website information provided in the Reference section was correct when provided by the author. The publisher can accept no responsibility for this information becoming incorrect.

CONTENTS

ORIGINS & HISTORY

The first Rangers, lightly equipped troops who 'ranged' deep in hostile territory and conducted what in modern terms are described as special operations, were primarily – although not exclusively – a phenomenon that developed in colonial America and reached their greatest expression in the wars of the mid-eighteenth century. The Seven Years War (1756–63) was truly global in scope and one of its main theatres was North America, where the French were steadily pushing southward from New France, their colonies in Canada, and thereby threatening British possessions along the New England seaboard. In attempting to stem the French tide the regular British Army was pitched into a style of fighting for which it was largely unprepared. In a densely wooded, often mountainous, terrain criss-crossed by numerous rivers, traditional set-piece battles between large formed bodies of rival troops were rare. The complex drills the ordinary soldier had learnt by rote, which also stifled any personal initiative, were far too rigid and inflexible for the conditions encountered. The French adapted their tactics to the conditions more readily by making extensive use of friendly Native Americans, and bands of French frontiersmen known as *coureurs du bois*, to conduct fast-moving hit-and-run raids, reconnaissance missions and ambushes. Their marksmanship, woodland and hunting skills, self-reliance and individual initiative proved much more suited to the terrain over which the campaign was conducted. Evidence of Britain's weakness was first revealed in July 1755 when a 1,400-strong column of British and colonial troops under Major-General Edward Braddock was virtually annihilated at the Battle of Monongahela in an ambush by 900 French and Native Americans.

Below: Major Robert Rogers (1731–95) of the British Army unit from which today's Rangers trace their lineage. In 1758 he was promoted to command His Majesty's Independent Companies of American Rangers – always known as Rogers' Rangers.

RANGERS IN COLONIAL AMERICA

Although the British were stung into creating units of light infantry from their own regular units to match the French after Monongahela, they also turned to the American colonists who had a long tradition of irregular frontier fighting. In 1675 during King Philip's War, a revolt by Metacomet of the Wampanoag tribe in Rhode Island over hunting and fishing rights, Captain Benjamin Church of Massachusetts formed a body of troops to deal with the unrest. The unit was known as Church's Rangers as its men 'ranged' far and wide to track down (and eventually kill) Metacomet. Typically, recruits to Church's Rangers and its descendants were hunters and frontiersmen, men skilled in living off the land who had often learned their skills from the Native Americans and often used them against the very same Native Americans in times of frontier unrest. Several more such units were raised during later periods of unrest, including Major John

Gorham's Company of Rangers. This New England unit first saw action during King George's War (1740–48), the North American offshoot of the European War of the Austrian Succession. Gorham's company comprised 50 or so Mohicans and frontiersmen and was chiefly involved in maintaining a British presence in Nova Scotia by quelling unrest among French settlers and Native Americans. The unit's importance was soon recognized – it doubled in size, Gorham received a regular commission in King George II's army and the Rangers received the same pay as British troops. The unit continued to serve in Nova Scotia, despite the death of John Gorham in 1751, and then participated in the French and Indian Wars under John's brother Joseph. Again it proved invaluable, taking part in the capture of Louisbourg, a key French fortress at the entrance to the St. Lawrence River, in 1758 and serving with Brigadier-General James Wolfe during the decisive Battle of the Plains of Abraham outside Quebec in 1759. Subsequently Gorham's Rangers took part in the attempt to storm Havana, Spain's chief colonial outpost in the New World, during 1762, and the following year participated in the quelling of the rebellion around Detroit led by Pontiac, leader of the Ottawa.

Although Gorham's Rangers was probably the most successful unit of the period, the founder of the most famous Ranger unit of the mid-eighteenth century was Robert Rogers (1731–95), a Massachusetts-born hunter, explorer and frontiersman, who in March 1756 was promoted to captain and given command of a unit known as the Ranger Company of Blanchard's New Hampshire Regiment. In 1758 he was again promoted, this time to major, and made commander of nine such companies, which were officially titled His Majesty's Independent Companies of American Rangers but were invariably known as Rogers' Rangers. The unit first saw action in an unsuccessful expedition to take Louisbourg in 1757 but was subsequently largely based at Fort Edward on the Hudson River some 60 miles (96km) north of Albany. It was from this base that Rogers conducted several

STANDING ORDERS
Rogers' Rangers

1. Don't forget nothing.
2. Have your musket clean as a whistle, hatchet scoured, sixty rounds of powder and ball, and be ready to march at a minute's notice.
3. When you're on the march, act the way you would if you was sneaking up on a deer. See the enemy first.
4. Tell the truth about what you see and what you do. There is an army depending on us for correct information. You can lie all you please when you tell other folks about the Rangers, but don't never lie to a Ranger or officer.
5. Don't never take a chance you don't have to.
6. When we're on the march we march single file, far enough apart so one shot can't go through two men.
7. If we strike swamps, or soft ground, we spread out abreast, so it's hard to track us.
8. When we march, we keep moving till dark, so as to give the enemy the least possible chance at us.
9. When we camp, half the party stays awake while the other half sleeps.
10. If we take prisoners, we keep 'em separate till we have had time to examine them, so they can't cook up a story between 'em.
11. Don't ever march home the same way. Take a different route so you won't be ambushed.
12. No matter whether we travel in big parties or little ones, each party has to keep a scout 20 yards ahead, 20 yards on each flank and 20 yards in the rear, so the main body can't be surprised and wiped out.
13. Every night you'll be told where to meet if surrounded by a superior force.
14. Don't sit down to eat without posting sentries.
15. Don't sleep beyond dawn. Dawn's when the French and Indians attack.
16. Don't cross a river by a regular ford.
17. If somebody's trailing you, make a circle, come back onto your own tracks, and ambush the folks that aim to ambush you.
18. Don't stand up when the enemy's coming against you. Kneel down, lie down, hide behind a tree.
19. Let the enemy come till he's almost close enough to touch. Then let him have it and jump out and finish him up with your hatchet.

Above: Rogers' Rangers Standing Orders of 1759 are still given to today's Ranger cadets.

missions that typified the Rangers' role and its dangers. In March 1758, he led a 180-strong force to reconnoitre French activity around Fort Ticonderoga, some 40 miles (65 km) north of Fort Edward. Initially moving by night, and despite appalling weather, the Rangers made good progress until confronted by around 100 Native Americans, a scouting party for a larger force of some 600 French-Canadians and other Native Americans. The Rangers ambushed the scouts, killing 40 or so, but then had to conduct a fighting withdrawal that cost 50 men.

A second operation, beginning on September 13, 1759, saw Rogers lead 200 Rangers against the pro-French Abenaki, who were encamped at St. Francis near the St. Lawrence River around 40 miles (64km) south of Montreal. The Rangers had to travel 300 miles (480km) through hostile and inhospitable terrain to reach their target. Setting out by boat from Crown Point on the west shore of Lake Champlain, Rogers' force travelled by night to avoid detection, resting during the day, and reached Missisquoi Bay undetected after 10 days. However, their numbers had been depleted by around 25 percent due to the accidental explosion of a gunpowder barrel. Rogers now hid his boats and moved towards St. Francis on foot, but two days later learned that the French had found his transports and were in hot pursuit. He nevertheless decided to continue and 12 days later reached St. Francis. Early the next morning he attacked the village and in a little more than an hour the Rangers killed more than 200 Abenaki, destroyed St. Francis, and rescued five captives for the loss of just one man. The return journey proved to be an epic of endurance. Short of supplies and harassed by the enemy, the Rangers split into several smaller groups to avoid detection. Some headed directly for Crown Point, while others made for a pre-agreed rendezvous point on the Ammonoosuck River. When Rogers stumbled in, there were no supplies as expected because the relief force had withdrawn just two hours before his arrival. A single Ranger officer and a young Native American were despatched by raft to a post known as Number Four some 100 miles (160 km) to the south and 10 days later returned with supplies. The Rangers' ordeal was over but the punitive expedition against the Abenaki had cost Rogers all but 93 of his men.

Following the end of the French and Indian Wars the Ranger concept went into decline until it was revived by both sides during the American War of Independence (1775–83). Chief among the British units to see service were the Queen's Rangers, originally a battalion of Loyalists led for a time by Rogers until his dismissal for unreliability fuelled by alcoholism in 1777. Rogers was replaced by a British officer, John Graves Simcoe, who turned the unit, which became known as Simcoe's Rangers, into a first-rate force that fought in several campaigns until forced into surrender at Yorktown in 1781. A second

Below: Colonel John S. Mosby's Confederate 43rd Battalion of Virginia Cavalry was the most successful guerrilla unit of the Civil War – so much so that part of north Virginia was dubbed 'Mosby's Confederacy'.

Above: Mosby's guerrillas in action. They tied down a great number of troops by effective harassment of Union supply lines.

battalion of Queen's Rangers was also raised and commanded by Robert Rogers' younger brother, James. It, too, saw extensive service in New York and around Lake Champlain.

Opposing the British were a number of pro-independence Ranger units raised at the instigation of the Continental Congress in June 1775. Two years later, Daniel Morgan was placed in charge of the Corps of Rangers, detachments of which fought with distinction at the Battles of Freeman's Farm (1777) and Cowpens (1781). At Freeman's Farm, part of the Battle of Saratoga, the defeated British commander, General John Burgoyne, remarked that Morgan's unit was 'the most famous corps in the Continental Army, all of them crack shots.' Morgan's exploits were matched by forces in South Carolina led by Francis Marion, known as the 'Swamp Fox' due to his elusiveness. Although not strictly Rangers, they undertook guerrilla missions that were recognizable in the tradition and proved a thorn in the side of both the British and their Loyalist allies.

RANGERS IN THE NINETEENTH CENTURY

The history of Ranger units in the nineteenth century paralleled that of the previous 100 years. Units were raised during periods of conflict and then swiftly disbanded once the fighting had ended. At the outbreak of the War of 1812 Congress ordered the raising of both foot and horse-mounted Rangers to protect the country's northern frontier from incursions by the British from Canada. Seventeen companies had been raised by the end of the war in 1815. For much of the remainder of the nineteenth century the need to protect the US frontier from outside aggression gave way to participating in the

expansion of the United States. Rangers fought in various campaigns against Native Americans, such as the wars against the Seminoles in Florida and, most famously, protected Americans living in the Mexican colony of Texas. Here, from 1823, Stephen Austin ordered the raising of an all-volunteer and unpaid mounted force that became known as the Texas Rangers. Aside from protecting American homesteaders and farmers, hunting down outlaws and maintaining the rule of law, the Texas Rangers undertook valuable scouting duties during the successful struggle to break away from Mexican rule in 1835–36 and the subsequent and successful war initiated by the United States against Mexico (1846–48) that led to the annexation of much of the southwest. Ranger units under officers such as Ben McCulloch and Jack Hays conducted forward reconnaissance missions for regular US forces during operations within Mexico.

The Texas Rangers and similar units also took part in the American Civil War (1861–65) and chiefly fought for the Confederacy. One of the earliest such units was Terry's Texas Rangers, which was raised by Benjamin Terry and Thomas Lubbock in 1861. Terry's men fought west of the Mississippi but similar units operated in the eastern theatre, most raised after the Confederate Congress enacted the Partisan Ranger Act in April 1862. Many of the units raised proved ill-disciplined and havens for criminals. Most were disbanded when the act was repealed in 1864, but some proved of continued value to the southern cause. Chief among these was the 43rd Virginia Cavalry, a unit commanded by John Singleton Mosby that was popularly known as Mosby's Rangers or Raiders. Mosby's daring exploits – raids and reconnaissance missions behind Union lines – earned him the nickname the 'Grey Ghost'. One of his most successful was a night raid against Fairfax Court House in northern Virginia during March 1863 that led to the capture of a brigadier general,

Edwin Stoughton, and severely embarrassed the Northern authorities. An attack on a Union railroad the following year caused similar embarrassment when it netted Mosby $170,000 originally destined to pay Northern troops. The Confederate raider and his band began to operate so effectively in northern Virginia that part of that state was christened 'Mosby's Confederacy' and, despite the best efforts of Northern forces, he remained at large throughout the war. He undertook his last mission on the day of the Confederate surrender at Appomattox Court House on April 9, 1865, and only formally disbanded his unit on the 21st.

The end of the Civil War was followed by a sustained westward drive that saw US citizens, many recent immigrants, settle in territories occupied by Native Americans. Clashes were inevitable, and the small peacetime US Army was quickly overstretched and not wholly suited to such a type of warfare. Once again Ranger-style units were formed to conduct scouting missions and hit-and-run raids against Native American villages. Many legendary figures of the Wild West participated in such campaigns, often as scouts, and among them were William Cody, better known as 'Buffalo Bill', and 'Texas' Jack Crawford. Larger bodies were also raised, such as the 50-strong Forsyth's Scouts raised by Major George Forsyth in 1868, but by the late 1880s the need for such formations was all but over due to the completion of the pacification programme directed against the Native Americans. The end of the Native American Wars left the Rangers and similar bodies with little to do. Some, such as the Texas Rangers continued to undertake law enforcement duties, but they had no obvious military role and the concept remained dormant for some 60 years until the outbreak of World War II.

REVIVING THE RANGER CONCEPT

The origin of the modern US Rangers lay with the Commando forces raised in Britain from 1940. President Roosevelt's enthusiasm for this type of force was communicated to the Chief of Staff of the US Army, General George Marshall, and he sent Colonel Lucian K. Truscott Jr. to England in early 1942 to evaluate the potential of Britain's Commando force and investigate the raising of similar US units. Not all the branches of the US armed forces were enthused by the idea. The Navy in general, and the Marine Corps in particular, felt that they had little to learn from the British and argued that they already had the training and capabilities to conduct the types of operation undertaken by the Commandos. This to some extent was true, as the Marine Corps was somewhat reluctantly raising specialist raider-type units to conduct such missions, but these Marine Raider battalions were largely needed in the Pacific, where the Japanese were posing a more immediate and ongoing threat.

Truscott, who was attached to the British Combined Operations staff under Lord Louis Mountbatten while in England, reported back to Marshall in late May and recommended the formation of a US Commando-type unit. The chief of staff concurred and the relevant orders to raise an 'American Commando' were issued on June 1. However, the chief of the general staff's Operations Division, Major General Dwight D. Eisenhower, pointed out that the name Commando was very much associated with the British and requested that a more American name be used for the new unit. Truscott remembered the exploits of Rogers and his men and suggested that Ranger would be a fitting alternative. With a name settled on, it was now necessary to find and train the officers and men for the reborn Rangers. The most immediate and accessible source of recruits were the US forces already stationed in Britain.

Above: General Ben McCulloch (1811–62) – once of the Texas Rangers – was killed at the Battle of Pea Ridge, Arkansas, in March 1862, while in command of the Confederates' west wing. His early war experiences were as a Texas Ranger, and as the captain of a Ranger company in the Mexican War; he would become Chief of Scouts to General Zachary Taylor. Known for his daring exploits, his reputation ensured his prominence during the Civil War. He was promoted general – the first Confederate to be elevated to this position from civilian life – and on August 10, 1861, he beat the forces of Brig. Gen. Nathaniel Lyon at Wilson's Creek in southwest Missouri. Fighting under Van Dorn at Pea Ridge, his troops overran a battery of Union artillery. McCulloch rode forward to get a better view of the enemy line, was shot from his horse and died instantly.

Left: John S. Mosby (1833–1916) after promotion to brigadier general.

READY FOR WAR

The officer designated to found the new Ranger unit was Major William O. Darby, an aide to Major General Russell P. Harte, commander of the US 34th Infantry Division and, from January 27, 1942, the head of the US Army Northern Ireland. Darby, an Arkansas-born West Point graduate whose chosen army career was in the artillery, was stationed at Carrickfergus, some 20 miles (32 km) north of Belfast, but had already requested more active assignments. On June 8 he was ordered to form a Commando-style unit but in the early summer of 1942 the US forces in Britain were small compared to what they would become by 1944. Nevertheless Darby set about raising suitable recruits from what was available locally. These were the two divisions that comprised the US V Corps, the 34th Infantry and 1st Armored, and various support units.

COMMANDO TRAINING AT ACHNACARRY

Over the following days Darby interviewed potential recruits, both officers and men, and by the 19th, the day that the 1st Ranger Battalion was officially activated, he had a pool of some 2,000 personnel to work with. These were quickly whittled down to around 570 men – 20 percent above the official establishment figure of 26 officers and 447 other ranks – but Darby expected many volunteers to fall by the wayside during training. The raw materials Darby had to work with were of many backgrounds and came from across the United States. The largest group, some 60 percent, had been serving with the 34th Division, and were mainly from Iowa, Minnesota and Nebraska. A further 30 percent were drawn from the 1st Armored Division and the remaining 10 percent were mainly support troops from V Corps' medical, logistical and signal units. On the 25th Darby and his recruits were inspected by General Robert Laycock, the commander of the British 1st Special Service Brigade, an experienced Commando group under whose direction the Rangers would receive their initial specialist training.

The Rangers transferred to the west coast of Scotland three days later and were based at Achnacarry Castle, a few miles north of Fort William close to Loch Arkaig. Achnacarry was home to the British Commando Training Depot and its commanding officer, Lieutenant-Colonel Charles Vaughan, was tasked with directing the Rangers' training programme. Vaughan, a long-serving officer with recent experience of the Commando raids on the Lofoten Islands and Vaagsø in northern Norway, had created a demanding and realistic course. The programme he had devised consisted of three parts and was undertaken by both officers and men. First, speed marches over the area's rugged mountains and valleys, which grew from three to 16 miles (5–25 km), coupled with timed obstacle courses built up the Rangers' strength and stamina. Next, they were shown how to use the weapons and equipment appropriate to lightly equipped raiding

Above: Corporal Franklin M. Koons (nicknamed 'Zip') was the first US soldier to kill a German in World War II during the landings at Dieppe in August 1942.

forces. Finally, they were taught the tactical skills they would need to carry out their specialist role, such as scouting and patrolling, silent killing, mountaineering, river-crossing and street-fighting. Three-day exercises were used to evaluate the Rangers. By the end of the first week Darby's original 20 percent surfeit of recruits had turned to a 10 percent deficit as many men fell by the wayside and were returned to their original units.

The Achnacarry training ended in late July and on August 1 the Rangers retraced their steps to Fort William to begin the next state of their preparations – amphibious warfare training directed by the Royal Navy. This was conducted at HMS *Dorlin*, a shore establishment near Acharacle on the coast of Argyll and ideally placed to make use of the adjacent Western Isles. The six Ranger companies were billeted in pairs at Glenborrodale, Glencripesdale and Roshven, while Darby set up his headquarters at Shielbridge. Early training centred on Kentra beach close to *Dorlin*, where the British had established a realistic course to test the Rangers' abilities with assault boats. Other skills developed included navigation, cliff assault and raids on coastal batteries. Once again, three-day exercises were used to put theory into practice.

BLOODING AT DIEPPE

It was during this period that a handful of Rangers gained first-hand experience of real combat. Operation Jubilee, the raid on the port of Dieppe on August 18–19, was designed to test the strength of the German defences in northern France and the feasibility of seizing a port, which was seen as an essential prerequisite for any future large-scale invasion of Nazi-occupied Europe. Although the bulk of the forces committed to Jubilee were drawn from the Canadian 2nd Division, it was planned as an all-arms operation, one involving 237 warships and some 74 squadrons of aircraft. A number of

This page: More views of training emphasising the skills needed to become a Ranger – physical endurance; climbing skills; unarmed and armed combat. Most of the early photos, such as these, were taken in Scotland as British Commando instructors (seen far right) put the Rangers through their paces – including jumping off the remarkable 20-foot (6m) barrier on the Commando assault course in Argyll (below right) with full pack, M1917A1 helmet and M1 rifle! Many of the Rangers' exercises were conducted using live firing to ensure the most realistic possible training environment. The preponderance of training photos of Rangers – and all special forces – against action shots is caused by the very nature of their missions. They tended to take place at night or in low light conditions, often in situations where a Press or Service photographer would have been a hindrance.

DIEPPE

The first American ground forces to see action against the Germans, three Rangers were killed (*) and several captured. Those of the 1st Ranger Battalion who took part were: 1-Lt. Leonard F. Dirks, 1-Lt. Robert Flanagan, 2-Lt. Charles M. Shunstrom, 2-Lt. Edwin V. Loustalot*, 2-Lt. Joseph H. Randall*, Capt. Roy A. Murray, S/Sgt. Gino Mercuriali, S/Sgt. Kenneth D. Stempson, S/Sgt. Lester E. Kness, S/Sgt. Merritt M. Bertholf, Sgt. Albert T. Jacobsen, Sgt. Alex Szima, Sgt. Dick Sellers, Sgt. Edwin C. Thompson, Sgt. Harold R. Adams, Sgt. John J. Knapp, Sgt. Kenneth G Kenyon, Sgt. Lloyd N. Church, Sgt. Marcell G Swank, Sgt. Marvin L. Kavanaugh, Sgt. Mervin T. Heacock, Sgt. Theodore Q. Butts, Sgt. Tom Sorby, T/4 Howard W. Henry*, T/5 Joe C. Phillips, T/5 John H. Smith, T/5 Michael Kerecman, T/5 William S. Brinkley, Cpl. Franklin M. Koons, Cpl. William R. Brady, Pfc. Charles F. Grant, Pfc. Charles R. Coy, Pfc. Charles Reilly, Pfc. Clare P. Beitel, Pfc. Donald G Johnson, Pfc. Donald L. Hayes, Pfc. Edwin R. Furru, Pfc. Erwin J. Moger, Pfc. Howard T. Hedenstad, Pfc. Howard W. Andre, Pfc. James C. Mosely, Pfc. James O. Edwards, Pfc. Owen E. Sweazey, Pfc. Pete M. Preston, Pfc. Stanley Bush, Pfc. Walter A. Bresnahan, Pfc. William E. Lienhas, Pfc. William S. Girdley, Pvt. Don A. Earwood, Pvt. Jacque M. Nixon.

Commando units were also deployed as was a small detachment of Rangers — 44 men and five officers under Captain Roy Murray. Also on hand was Truscott, who acted as an observer.

The bulk of the Rangers were attached to the two British Commandos that were earmarked to neutralize the German coastal batteries to the east and west of Dieppe. Forty Rangers including Murray were assigned to No. 3 Commando under Lieutenant-Colonel J.F. Durnford-Slater and this force sailed from Newhaven on the south coast of England late on the 18th. Their mission was to come ashore at two beaches codenamed Yellow 1 and Yellow 2 some five miles (8 km) to the east of Dieppe and then silence the cliff-top battery at Bruneval, which had been designated 'Goebbels'. The Commandos and Rangers crossed the English Channel in 27 slow-moving wooden landing craft known as Eurekas as part of a flotilla that included *Steam Gun Boat No. 5*, with Durnford-Slater and Murray on board, *Motor Launch 348* and an anti-aircraft vessel.

The plan was soon in disarray. Four of the Eurekas turned back because of engine failure and the remainder then ran into a small German convoy some 8 miles (13 km) from their target at around 0347 hours on the 19th. In the subsequent firefight many of the Eurekas suffered heavy damage, were sunk or dispersed, and the steam gun boat was virtually wrecked. Durnford-Slater and Murray were therefore unable to play any further part in Jubilee. Only one Eureka reached the target area on schedule but its men could do little more than direct harassing fire against Goebbels battery before withdrawing after some 90 minutes. Six other Eurekas did make a landing but they were 25 minutes late and the troops came ashore in daylight. Some 50 men, including a handful of Rangers, were soon pinned down by heavy fire and were unable to make any progress inland. One of the Rangers, Lieutenant Edwin Loustalot, was mortally wounded, becoming the first US soldier to be killed in European land fighting during World War II. The remainder of the party were eventually taken prisoner.

The attack on the coastal battery codenamed 'Hess' some six miles (10 km) to the west of Dieppe was led by Lord Lovat's No. 4 Commando, which included six Rangers (four sergeants and two corporals), and proved much more successful. Their crossing in

HMS *Prince Albert*, a converted ferry, was uneventful and two assault parties, known as Group One and Group Two, were successfully landed around Varengeville-sur-Mer. Lord Lovat led Group Two ashore at a beach codenamed Orange 2, which lay some 2 miles (3 km) from Group One's target, Orange 1. This pincer attack against Hess was conducted with surprise and great speed and the defenders were quickly overwhelmed and the battery neutralized. One of the Rangers, Corporal Franklin Koons, became the first US soldier to kill a German in combat and his sniping skills during the action earned him a Military Medal, which was presented by Lord Louis Mountbatten, head of Britain's Combined Operations. By 0730 the action was over and Lovat's men were withdrawn without difficulty.

The action against Hess was the only clear-cut success of the whole controversial operation. The main landing by the Canadians stalled on the beaches and ended in heavy losses – some 3,400 men or close to 70 percent of those engaged – but Jubilee did highlight shortcomings in equipment and tactics for amphibious warfare. The Rangers also suffered in this learning process. Darby recorded seven officers and men missing in action – either killed or taken prisoner – and seven injured. Consequently four officers and 39 men returned from the Dieppe raid and their experiences were used to improve the battalion's amphibious training. Despite Jubilee's failure, the Rangers' role in the operation made front-page news in the United States. The *New York Post* led with the banner headline 'We Land in France' while the *New York World Telegram* somewhat optimistically proclaimed that 'US Troops Smash the French Coast'.

PREPARING FOR OPERATION TORCH

The Rangers' time at HMS *Dorlin* came to an end shortly after the Dieppe raid and they moved from the west to east coast of Scotland. At Dundee, they were partnered with the British No. 1 Commando to undertake joint training that emphasized techniques for neutralizing all manner of coastal defences, such as batteries and pill boxes. The programme lasted until September 24, when the 1st Battalion boarded a train that took it to Glasgow. The Rangers were assigned to the US II Corps and attached to the US 1st Infantry Division. Both the division and Darby's men had been earmarked to play a leading role in the forthcoming invasion of North Africa, Operation Torch, which was scheduled to open in early November. Between September 29 and October 25, the Rangers honed the skills they had been taught over the previous months and were given some final lessons on the best way of loading both themselves and their equipment into assault craft of various types. On the 26th the months of preparation came to an end. After travelling to Gourock, a few miles west of Glasgow, the battalion boarded three former Glasgow–Belfast ferries, the *Royal Scotsman*, *Royal Ulsterman* and *Ulster Monarch*, which had been commandeered by the Royal Navy as amphibious assault transports and were preparing to take them to North Africa.

Above: Another view of 'Zip' Koons, who gained fame for his fighting at Dieppe; note the 1st Rangers shoulder flash.

Left: 1st Ranger Battalion exercise on a wet autumn day in Scotland, October 31, 1942 – one of a series of photographs taken on this exercise (see also pages 18, 19 and 68).

Above and Opposite: Landing craft training, Scotland October 31, 1942.

Left: Well it started fine! Preparing kit for their next exercise, men of 1st Rangers, October 9, 1942.

IN ACTION

OPERATION TORCH – THE INVASION OF NORTH AFRICA

The 1st Ranger Battalion was assigned to Major General Lloyd Fredendall's Centre Task Force for Operation Torch. Fredendall's overall role was to seize the port of Oran in Algeria in a widely dispersed three-pronged assault and, aside from the Rangers, his command included the US 1st Armored and 1st Infantry Divisions. Darby's men were assigned to spearhead the easternmost of Fredendall's three landings by combat teams drawn from the 1st Infantry Division on beaches near the small port of Arzew some 25 miles (40 km) east of Oran. Darby's chief task was to neutralize two Vichy French coastal batteries that could potentially devastate the assault craft carrying the two of the 1st Division's regimental combat teams that were scheduled to land at three beaches codenamed Z Green, Z White and Z Red in Arzew Bay to the immediate southeast of Arzew itself. One battery, known as Fort de la Pointe, was sited at the harbour's northern edge and contained three coastal guns surrounded by barbed wire and behind which lay a small French fort with walls about 20 feet (6 m) high. The second and potentially more threatening target, the Batterie du Nord, containing four 105 mm guns, was on high ground north of the fort and overlooked both the harbour and Arzew Bay. Darby formulated a plan of attack after studying air photographs of his objectives and the area surrounding Arzew. He opted to split his command into two groups and assault the batteries simultaneously, thereby capitalizing on the element of surprise. A smaller group under Major Herman Dammer was ordered to sail directly into Arzew harbour to tackle the Fort de la Pointe while the larger party under Darby himself was to come ashore some four miles (6 km) north of the Batterie du Nord and attack it from the rear.

Late on November 7, as the Centre Task Force's ships sailed eastward some 15 miles (24 km) offshore toward Arzew Bay and rounded Cap Carbon, *Ulster Monarch* and *Royal Ulsterman* with Darby's four Ranger companies – C, D, E and F – on board dropped out of the convoy and followed the coastline due south to the small landing beach north of the Batterie du Nord that had previously been identified from the air photographs. Nearing their target under cover of darkness and a sea fog, the Rangers embarked in 10 Landing Craft, Assault, which were backed by a pair of Landing Craft, Support. One of the assault craft became stuck in its davits, pitching its occupants into the waters below. All were quickly rescued and the remaining craft headed for shore, although they had to be guided in by the captain of the *Ulster Monarch*, who had spotted that they were initially heading in the wrong direction. This last-minute course correction allowed the Rangers to reach their allocated beach, land undetected save for a surprised and easily captured French sentry, and then quickly scale the cliff that

Below: Lieutenant Colonel William O. Darby on a speed march with his men, December 5, 1942, North Africa (see biography page 81).

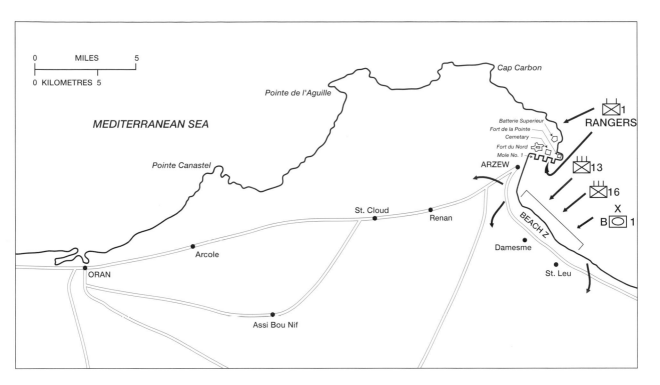

barred their exit from the beach. Darby's assault group moved towards its objective by following the coast road to within two miles (3 km) of the battery and then followed a wadi that led to the ridge line on top of which lay the Batterie du Nord and a smaller supporting defensive work called the Fort du Nord.

As Darby made his way toward his target, the two Ranger companies that had remained with the main invasion force sailing toward Arzew disembarked into five assault craft from the *Royal Scotsman* at 0100 hours on the 8th. Christened Dammer Force, the men of Companies A and B headed for shore in silence. Finding the boom that might have delayed their attack open rather than closed as expected, they sailed undetected and on schedule into the harbour – but on the wrong course. A swift realignment brought them back on track and they made their way between the outer jetty and main pier as planned. Moments later the assault craft reached a low but slanting seawall and their ramps came down, leaving the Rangers to scramble noisily over the slippery sea defences with some difficulty and then make their way to the battery. Surprise was total despite the noise. Three Vichy French soldiers were captured at gunpoint as the Rangers made their approach and the barbed wire surrounding the Fort de la Pointe was swiftly cut. The attackers bounded over a low wall, fired a few shots to make their presence known, and within 15 minutes had captured the guns and around 60 prisoners.

Darby now commenced his assault against the Batterie du Nord. Company D with four 81 mm mortars was deployed in a convenient ditch some 500 yards (500 m) from the battery to provide covering fire while Companies C, F and E approached its northern perimeter and began cutting paths through the 14-foot (4 m) wide barbed wire entanglements that skirted the position. As this task was being completed the Vichy French opened fire with several machine guns that threatened the momentum of the attack. Darby called down mortar fire and, after just eight highly accurate rounds, the French fire died away and the Rangers stormed into the compound. Some headed for the battery's control tower, others thrust bangalore torpedoes into the barrels of the coastal

Above: The Rangers' landings at Arzew, North Africa, November 8, 1942. It wasn't the largest operation the Rangers would take part in during the war, but it was handled efficiently and the objectives were taken.

Right and Opposite: Operation Torch – the assault craft, November 8, 1942. The photo on page 23 is on either *Ulster Monarch* or *Royal Ulsterman* and shows 81mm mortar rounds being loaded into an assault craft preparatory to the attack. Note the US flag and white armbands (see also photos on page 24). These were worn to identify friendly forces during the attack.

Opposite, Below: Physical exercise on board the transport during the journey to North Africa, November 5, 1942.

Below: Training continued, even in Africa; this shows Rangers preparing to assault a gun position, December 12, 1942. Most of the Rangers spent the end of 1942 and the beginning of 1943 attached to 5th Army Invasion Training Center at Arzew where they took part in exercises as demonstration troops. This is part of the area assaulted in earnest on November 8. Note the fixed bayonets: the Rangers often used the M1 rifle and M1905 bayonet.

Above: The official caption identifies this as forcing the doors on a building captured during the fighting on November 8. The general lack of interest exhibited by the troops shows that the action was over by this time. Note the white identification armbands in this and the photograph below.

guns, while others stormed though the position's main entrance. The bulk of the garrison had taken shelter in an underground powder store and, after being threatened by grenades and bangalore torpedoes thrown down its ventilator shafts, they surrendered. The battery was securely in Darby's hands by 0400 hours at a cost of two Rangers killed and eight wounded and he was able to signal his success to the invasion fleet lying offshore.

As the main landings got underway around Arzew the Rangers conducted various mopping-up operations around the batteries and harbour. At dawn Darby turned his attentions to the Fort du Nord. Vichy machine guns opened fire as he was attempting to persuade the garrison to surrender by telephone but Darby was able to secure the fort commander's agreement as Ranger mortar fire struck the position and silenced the fire. Darby and a small party of his men moved towards their objective but once again machine guns opened up on them and a Ranger company decided to force the issue by assaulting the fort. Some men were halted by its moat but others stormed across the drawbridge and broke through the main gateway. The garrison surrendered immediately and the Rangers marched them away to the Batterie du Nord. Meanwhile, after neutralizing the Batterie de la Pointe, Dammer Force fanned out to occupy key points, such as the small oil refinery north of the harbour, and dealt with Vichy snipers who were harassing the Rangers. A hillside cemetery between the two forts was cleared before dawn and then the Rangers dealt with similar resistance in the harbour area, chiefly around the piers and warehouses, and silenced a battery of 75 mm field guns firing on Allied shipping.

Most of the Ranger companies remained in Arzew over the next three days to complete its pacification and maintain order, but two were detached to aid units from the 1st Infantry Division as its regimental combat teams pushed southeast and southwest from their landing beaches. Lieutenant Max Schneider's Company E moved out on the afternoon of the 8th to support the 1st Battalion, 16th Infantry Regiment's

push along the coast road running southeast from Arzew. The rendezvous took place at 0700 on the 9th and Schneider was ordered to move down the road towards the town of La Macta. Some 800 yards (700 m) east of Port-aux-Poules the company was hit by light fire from concealed positions on a low ridge. This was brushed aside and, after a successful enveloping attack just a mile from La Macta, Schneider's men captured their objective. Company C was first tasked with defending the headquarters of the 1st Division at the village of Tourville on the 8th but then aided the 1st Battalion, 18th Infantry Regiment, in its assault on St. Cloud some 12 miles (20 km) southwest of Arzew. The Rangers established blocking positions south of the town under cover of darkness but at dawn on the 9th were hit by intense enemy fire at close range. The company commander, Lieutenant Klefman, was killed but the St. Cloud garrison surrendered during the afternoon. Both detached companies returned to Arzew on the 10th.

The Rangers' role in Operation Torch, which had cost them a mere four killed and 11 wounded and led to the capture of several hundred prisoners, ended with the actions at La Macta and St. Cloud, and Darby's men were not initially involved in the subsequent, somewhat badly handled Allied drive eastward toward German-held Tunisia. For the next three months they were attached to the Fifth Army Invasion Training Center at Arzew, honing their own skills particularly in night fighting and teaching seaborne assault techniques to other units. At the end of January 1943 the battalion underwent some reorganization: Company D gave up its mortars and regained its purely assault role, while an entirely new Company G was formed from more than 100 fresh volunteers. The spell at the training centre ended at the beginning of February. On the 1st the battalion boarded 32 Douglas C-47 transports at Oran and was flown to Youks-les-Bains airfield near Tébessa close to the Algerian–Tunisian border.

Above: Full marching order for 1st Rangers as they march past agaves on December 5, 1942.

Below left: This is a photograph closer to the action. It shows Rangers in position on the Batterie du Nord on November 8 following the brief battle for Arzew. Note the M1919A4 Browning .30 machine gun, the standard support weapon for the Rangers.

THE BATTLE FOR TUNISIA

After landing, the Rangers moved to the headquarters of General Lloyd Fredendall, commander of the US II Corps, which lay a little to the east of Tébessa, and Darby was briefed on his next operations. The proposed missions had two aspects. First, to conduct a reconnaissance in strength to identify the Axis divisions, both Italian and German, that were retreating into central Tunisia from neighbouring Tripolitania along the coast by way of Gabès. Second, they were to mask the redeployment of Allied units away from southern and central Tunisia, to meet a thrust by Colonel-General Jürgen von Arnim's Fifth Panzer Army from Tunis and Bizerte in the north of the country, by conducting hit-and-run raids and aggressive patrols to mislead the enemy as to the real strength of the opposition they faced. Three raids were planned – against Italian positions some five miles (8 km) from Station de Sened, against the Djebel el Ank, and Medilla. Observation of the enemy at Sened revealed that the Rangers faced troops from two of the Italian Army's better formations – the *Centauro* Division and the Bersaglieri.

Darby began the first raid on February 11, setting out towards Sened, which lay some 32 miles (56 km) from the Rangers' encampment at Gafsa, at the head of half of the 1st Battalion – Companies A, E and F. The first 20 miles (32 km) were by truck and jeep but then the raiders dismounted at a front-line Free French outpost and conducted the final approach on foot. By dawn on the 12th they had covered some 8 miles (13 km) more and lay just four miles from their target. Darby ordered his men to hide up during daylight to avoid detection from enemy ground observers and reconnaissance aircraft, and laid plans for the attack. The final approach to Sened began at around midnight, and at 600 yards (550 m) distance Darby ordered his men into a skirmish line for the assault. The Rangers had so far been undetected but some 200 yards (200 m) from the target, the Italians opened fire with machine guns. Nevertheless, the attack caught most of Sened's garrison by surprise as Darby's men swept into the positions. Aided by mortar fire, the Rangers quickly overcame any opposition. Many of the Italians fled, but around 50 were killed and many more wounded. The Rangers, who had one man killed and 18 wounded, also captured 10 prisoners from the 10th Bersaglieri Regiment. With dawn on the 12th less than three hours away, Darby now ordered a rapid withdrawal. His command was divided into two columns, one of which included the wounded, and both set off on the 12-mile (20 km) trudge back to friendly lines. Both groups returned without further loss – the faster column arrived at dawn on the 12th and the slower with the wounded during the following day.

Sened was an operation of the type that had brought Robert Rogers' fame in the eighteenth century and its success was recognized by the awards given to the 1st Battalion. Darby, four of his fellow officers and nine enlisted men received the Silver Star; the Italians who had faced the

Below: The advance towards Kasserine, Tunisia 1943.

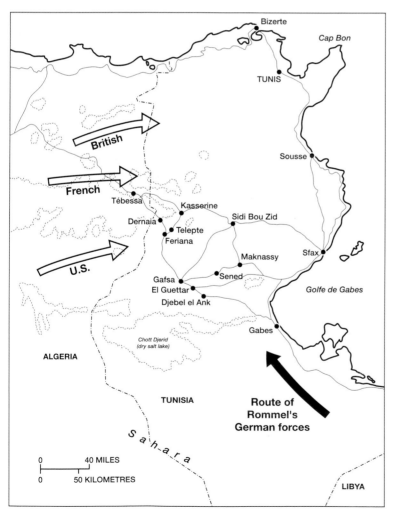

Rangers took to calling them the 'Black Death'.

However, the Rangers were unable to capitalize on their success at Sened as the other planned raids were cancelled due to a major two-pronged German attack that was launched against the Kasserine Pass in central Tunisia. Devised by Field Marshal Erwin Rommel, who had recently returned to North Africa after an illness, the intention was for armoured units to strike through the pass that ran through the Western Dorsale range, capture the Allied base at Tébessa and then turn northwards to encircle the Allied forces battling in northern Tunisia. The Rangers, who were acting as a rearguard, pulled out of Gafsa on the 14th and three days later they moved into position to cover the eastern entrance to Dernaia Pass, a second route south of Kasserine that also led to Tébessa. The Rangers were strung out over two miles (3 km) of front in hill-top positions some four miles (6 km) from the vital Gafsa–Kasserine road at Feriana from where a route branched westwards through the Dernaia Pass towards Tébessa. Axis troops were advancing along the Gafsa–Kasserine road and the Rangers were ideally placed to report on these troops' movements. The Germans did not assault Dernaia directly but kept it under periodic artillery fire and launched various probes and reconnaissance operations. The Rangers also conducted patrols and had firefights with the enemy but there were no major attacks to deal with, although one company was flung into the battle for Kasserine on the 22nd.

The Rangers remained at Dernaia Pass until March 1, when they were withdrawn from the front line and went into camp at Djebel Kouif. On the 13th they set out for Gafsa, some 50 miles (80 km) southeast of Dernaia, once again and reached the town three days later. Gafsa was the juncture of two important roads that led northeast and southeast through passes to the coast of central Tunisia and was to be the springboard for attacks by Patton's US II Corps after the end of the fighting at Kasserine. The northern advance towards Sfax by way of Sened and Maknassy was led by the US 1st Armored Division, while the US 1st Infantry Division and the 1st Rangers were tasked with capturing Axis-held El Guettar, from where roads lead northeast to Sfax and southeast to Gabès. The Rangers were ordered to probe El Guettar to discover the strength of the defences and on March 18 they moved against their objective under cover of darkness only to find that the oasis had been abandoned.

With El Guettar as a forward base, II Corps' attack towards the coast could develop and the Rangers were ordered to seize the commanding heights of Djebel el Ank, which overlooked the routes to Sfax and Gabès. These enemy positions were only five miles (8 km) from El Guettar, but were too strong to attack frontally, so Darby pulled his men back to Gafsa and launched them on a 12-mile (20 km) flanking march late on the evening

Above: The white armbands have gone as the Rangers march back from an exercise on December 5, 1942.

Above: Troop movement during the Battle of Sened. An extremely successful use of the Rangers saw the Italian troops at the Station de Sened in a surprise attack. Darby and thirteen other Rangers received Silver Stars for the action.

of the 20th. The lightly equipped Rangers made good progress, although the accompanying combat engineers with their heavy mortars found the going more difficult. By 0600 on the 13th Darby was ready to assault the enemy positions. The attack commenced, with the Rangers neutralizing enemy strongpoints one by one, often at bayonet point, despite facing heavy machine-gun and artillery fire. Two hours later the combat engineers began dropping mortar rounds on the remaining Axis emplacements. The main battle ended successfully in the early afternoon, when the US 1st Infantry Division's 26th RCT arrived to occupy the djebel, but the Rangers continued mopping-up operations until 1400 hours, when Darby was able to report the capture of both the heights and 200 prisoners.

The swift loss of Djebel el Ank brought about a series of counterattacks from the Germans, who immediately attacked the high ground stretching in a curve from the Djebel el Ank in the north to Djebel Berda, some five miles (8 km) south of the El Guettar–Gabès road, that was now occupied by the 1st Infantry Division. On the 24th the Rangers were moved to aid two battalions of the division's 18th Infantry Regiment which were struggling to beat off German counterattacks against their positions on the Djebel Berda. Darby's men initially settled down on the djebel's Hill 772 but all of the battalion bar Company D were flung into action against a German attack on the isolated battalions. For three days the Rangers fought on, often surrounded, but their action allowed the two battalions to withdraw in good order. The Rangers were relieved by units of the US 9th Infantry Division and withdrawn from the fighting around El Guettar on March 27, although the battle continued for several days. The 1st Battalion received a Presidential Unit Citation for this action some 12 months later.

Darby now found his battalion divided to undertake patrolling duties as the campaign in Tunisia entered its final phase. Two companies were stationed at Gafsa, two at Madjene el Fedj, some 25 miles (40 km) north, and two at Sidi bou Sid, a further 35 miles (56 km) to the north.

The last Axis forces in North Africa finally surrendered on May 13 but the Rangers had already departed to prepare for their next operation. On April 17 they had moved by road and rail to Nemours, close to Oran in Algeria, where the battalion established a base and training facilities. Two days later Darby, who had requested the expansion of the Rangers, was informed that he was to oversee the creation of two new battalions and that they had to be ready for action in six weeks. Darby decided to split his existing battalion into three two-company groups and use these experienced men as the core of the new units. As a 2nd Battalion had been activated in the United States on April 1, Companies A and B consequently formed the basis for the 3rd Rangers under Major Herman Dammer, Companies E and F went to the 4th Rangers under Major Roy Murray, while Companies C and D were used to rebuild the 1st Battalion under Darby. With time pressing, Darby scoured North Africa for potential recruits and candidates were despatched to Nemours to undergo training with Dammer. The two new units were formerly activated on May 21 but were given the title Provisional until June 21. The whole command, which was reinforced by the 83rd Chemical Mortar Battalion (equipped with 4.2-inch mortars), was designated the Ranger Force (Provisional) but was more commonly known as Darby's Rangers.

THE INVASION OF SICILY

Darby's Rangers had been detailed for a leading role in Operation Husky, the Anglo-US invasion of Sicily. The Rangers were earmarked to spearhead landings by the US Seventh Army under General George Patton at two points on the island's west coast – the towns of Licata and Gela. As the invasion drew near, Darby moved with the the 1st and 4th

While the Rangers were preparing for the invasion of Sicily, in the United States and United Kingdom other cadres were preparing. These photographs were taken on a wet February 26, 1943, at the Commando Depot (later the Commando Basic Training Centre), which had been established at Achnacarry Castle, near Fort William, in the Highlands of Scotland in March 1942. The depot was commanded by the formidable Lt-Col Charles Vaughan (see *Spearhead 10 Commandos*) who is in both photographs.

Above: Top brass at the Commando Depot watching 29th Rangers parade: from left to right in the front – Capt Joy, depot adjutant; J.M. Pate, Minister of War Transport; Maj Gen. Gerow; Brig. Robert Laycock, chief of the Special Service Brigade; and Lt-Col. Vaughan.

Left: Major-General Gerow talks to Sgt John O'Brien of the 29th Rangers. Nearest the camera is Lt-Col. Vaughan. (See also pages 44–45 for further information on 29th Ranger Battalion.)

Battalions to the vicinity of Algiers to link up with the 1st Infantry Division once again, while Dammer moved his command to camps around Bizerte in northern Tunisia to support Major General Lucian Truscott's US 3rd Infantry Division.

The 1st and 4th Rangers boarded the landing ships USS *Dickman*, HMS *Albert* and HMS *Charles*. They were to act as a spearhead force to tackle Axis defences at Gela before the main landing by the 1st Infantry Division began. Estimates suggested that the target and its environs were defended by three fixed shore batteries, a battery of 77 mm field guns, two mortar companies and more than a score of machine-gun positions. Darby planned for his two battalions to land directly opposite Gela, to the left and right of a 2,000-yard (1,800 m) pier that jutted out into the harbour from the dead centre of the coastal town. The 1st Rangers were to land to the north of the pier and then swing westward to neutralize a fort, while the 4th Rangers swung eastward to deal with other coastal defences. Half an hour after the initial assault the 1st Battalion, 39th Engineers, was scheduled to land on the 1st Rangers' beach to be followed at 30-minute intervals by the 83rd Chemical Mortar Battalion and a second battalion of engineers respectively. The 1st Battalion engineers, fighting as infantry, were ordered to fill the vacuum left by the flanking attacks of the two Ranger battalions.

At around 0130 hours on July 10, the Rangers clambered into their 48 assault craft from their landing ships, a task made difficult because of 40 mph (64 km/h) winds and rough waters, and headed for their forming up point some five miles (8 km) from their dropping-off point. The final run in, which took some 30 minutes, began at 0245. The enemy were alert to imminent attack but their fire, although heavy and directed by searchlights, was largely inaccurate and the Rangers made directly for shore with little difficulty. As expected the pier was primed for demolition and its central section was demolished just as the the attackers passed, but few casualties were caused and the assault waves made for shore, some arriving five minutes early. Many boats reached their allotted target without difficulty but others beached on sandbars and the Rangers had to wade ashore. Some made it easily but others, particularly in the 4th Battalion, became casualties when they ran into barbed wire and a minefield. The two battalions next moved through the edges of Gela, meeting only light resistance from occasional snipers, and then began the task of neutralizing the flanking defences. Aided by salvoes from the cruiser USS *Savannah*, the 1st Battalion quickly overcame the defenders of the fort, while similar successes were achieved by the 4th Rangers.

These missions complete, Darby reassembled his forces on the beaches and led them into Gela to form a perimeter to protect the ongoing unloading of troops and supplies. At around 0700 hours the Italians pushed tanks of their Gruppo Mobile E into the town and these were beaten off thanks to a single 37 mm anti-tank gun managed by Darby and Captain Charles Shunstrom, bazookas and satchel

Below: Gela was a significant target on the east of Seventh Army's landings on Sicily. The Rangers secured their objective, threw a perimeter around the city and held it against counter-attacks. This is the cathedral on July 11, 1943, the day after the landings.

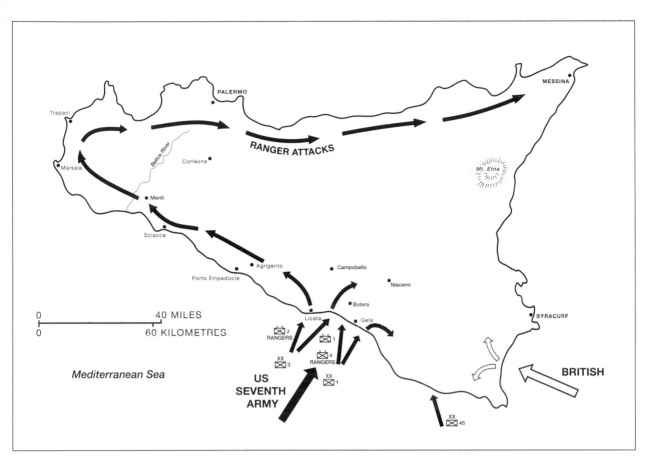

charges. A greater threat developed around midday, when 18 German tanks rumbled toward the town supported by elements of the Italian *Livorno* Division. Once again the attack was repulsed by the Rangers, who bolstered their own meagre fire power with rounds from the mortars, a number of captured 77 mm field guns, and offshore naval support. A third attack by a battalion of enemy infantry stalled some 2,000 yards (1,800 m) from the town thanks to the massed firepower of the 83rd Chemical Mortar Battalion. By early afternoon Gela was firmly held by the Allies and the Axis troops were withdrawing into the high ground around the town.

On the 12th Darby was ordered to advance towards San Nicola and Monte Delta Lapa, mountains that rise precipitously out of the coastal plain and guard the entrance to a pass some four miles (6 km) northwest of Gela that leads to Licata and its invasion beaches. As the 1st Infantry Division battled inland for the town of Niscemi, Darby moved against the enemy holding the peaks with a command reinforced by the engineer and mortar units that had landed with the Rangers two days previously and a newly attached armoured infantry detachment. The armoured infantry and engineers assaulted San Nicola while the two Ranger battalions struck against Monte Delta Lapa. Under cover of darkness the Rangers climbed the steep-sided peak but ran into a hail of artillery fire from concealed batteries. The attack stalled and only regained its momentum when Darby called down fire support from the *Savannah* that proved highly accurate. The Rangers took some 600 prisoners during the battle and linked up with the 3rd Division, which had been pushing southwards from Licata, the following day.

Darby's next task was to assault the inland town of Butera, some 4,000 feet (1,200 m) above sea level and eight miles (12 km) inland due north of Gela. Fire support

Above: The Rangers' Sicilian campaign, which started at Gela and Licata and ended on the coast opposite the toe of Italy.

was provided by 18 self-propelled 75 mm howitzers and the *Savannah*. The advance, a two-pronged attack, commenced under cover of darkness shortly after midnight. Some of the troops moving directly on Butera pushed forward at a rapid rate, forcing Darby to halt the imminent artillery bombardment. Although German officers attempted to force the Italians to fight, they had little success and the small party of Rangers occupied the town with unexpected ease.

While Darby was securing Gela and battling for Butera, Major Herman Dammer's 3rd Rangers had landed on beaches some three miles (5 km) west of Licata to the north of Gela, paving the way for the arrival of the US 3rd Infantry Division's 7th Regimental Combat Team. The first waves came ashore unhindered at 0400 on the 10th but quickly ran into sporadically heavy machine-gun and artillery fire from enemy positions on high ground. These were soon overcome and the battalion turned eastwards, moving along a ridge that ran directly into Licata itself. The town was quickly occupied and the battalion remained there until the morning of the 12th, when it advanced inland to Campobello to the north. Dammer's Rangers next moved via truck and on foot to first Naro and then Favara in the van of a northwards sweep to clear the coast of the enemy. From Favara the troops moved westwards towards the town of Agrigento, which was held by a sizeable Italian garrison.

The plan to capture Agrigento involved a regiment of the 3rd Division moving directly on the target while the Rangers tackled a high peak known as Montaperto, from where Axis artillery could fire down on any force moving on the town, as the first stage of a flank march around Agrigento. Some three miles (5 km) out of Favara the Rangers, who were attempting to clear a roadblock barring their way forwards, were struck by intense artillery fire, but they were able to break through the Italian defences and capture some 165 prisoners within the hour. The main attack on Montaperto opened on the morning of July 16 and, despite enemy artillery fire, the Rangers scrambled up the peak's steep slopes supported by their mortars. This fire forced the Italian gunners to abandon their artillery pieces and a fortuitous round also hit the battery's ammunition dump. Montaperto was quickly occupied and Dammer's men then swept over an adjoining piece of high ground, where the enemy had command and observation posts. Here, the Italians surrendered without a fight.

After the capture of Montaperto the Rangers again moved southward in the direction of Porto Empedocle, a coastal town lying just north of Agrigento. From positions in an almond grove some 2,000 yards (1,800 m) from the town, the battalion, minus one company left to guard the left flank and rear, launched a pincer attack from east and west at around 1430 on the 16th. While the the two companies under Dammer attacking from the east quickly overcame pockets of resistance, three companies under Major Alvah Miller had to fight hard to crush German troops holding a walled cemetery and coastal defence positions. Porto Empedocle was declared secure by 1600. On the 17th the 3rd Battalion established a camp near Montaperto but during the following day moved to Raffadalio north of Agrigento, where it remained for a week and then rejoined the rest of Darby's command, which was now based at Ribera, a few miles farther north.

Some seven days after the landings and initial exploitation phase of Husky, the Allies had control of several linked and expanding beachheads and were poised to drive through Sicily toward their ultimate objective – Messina. Patton's US Seventh Army in the western half of island was detailed to support the main drive by General Bernard Montgomery's British Eighth Army in the east. However, Montgomery encountered stubborn resistance that slowed his advance to a crawl and Patton, facing lesser opposition, decided to strike out for Palermo on the

Below: S/Sgt Francis P. Padrucco of 1st Rangers was awarded the Silver Star for his actions during the assault on Gela, Sicily. His left arm carries the 1st Ranger Battalion's shoulder flash; next the white 5 and A displayed on a blue field against a red background denoting Fifth Army; finally his staff sergeant's stripes.

island's northwest coast rather than relieve some of the pressure faced by the British. Several units, part of a newly activated Provisional Corps under Major General Geoffrey Keyes, were committed to the drive on Palermo. Darby was given command of Force X, which comprised the three Ranger battalions, the 39th Regimental Combat Team, and a battalion of 155 mm guns, and ordered to follow the coast road that looped round the northeast of the island.

Darby initially left his Ranger battalions close to Ribera and late on July 20 set off to locate the 39th RCT. After passing through Sciacca, he located the unit at Menfi at 0300 hours the following day and the advance along the coast began two hours later. The objective was to capture Castelvetrano and then march on Marsala

on the island's west tip before swinging due east to reach Palermo. The RCT successfully overcame Axis forces defending the line of the Belice River and Castelvetrano fell on the 22nd, the day that other US troops entered Palermo. With Palermo secured, the RCT, reinforced by the 1st and 4th Rangers, swept though northwest Sicily, taking Marsala and then liberating Trapani on the north coast some 40 miles (64 km) west of Palermo. Within a few days, Force X and the accompanying 82nd Airborne Division were in position around San Guiseppe to the south of Palermo, marking the end of the liberation of western Sicily. Force X was immediately disbanded.

While the 1st and 4th Battalions were placed in reserve and established a camp at Corleone to the south of Palermo, the 3rd Battalion, which had been held back at Menfi during the drive to clear western Sicily, moved up to the front and was attached to Truscott's 3rd Infantry Division for a second time. The division was pushing towards Messina on the northeast tip of the island and had reached Sant'Agata di Militello on the sole coastal road, Highway 113, between Palermo and Messina and some 50 miles (80 km) short of its objective. The 3rd Battalion, soon joined by Darby and a 1st Battalion company, served with the division's 7th Regimental Combat Team and was pitched into battle against German rearguards in the Caronie Mountains who were attempting to protect the ongoing withdrawal of forces from Messina to the Italian mainland by way of the Straits of Messina. On August 12 the Rangers first stormed the high ground of Popo di Marco, four miles (6 km) southwest of Capo d'Orlando, and then aided the drive of the 7th RCT towards Naso on Highway 113. The next target was Patti, some 35 miles (56 km) from Messina. For this operation the Rangers fought alongside the division's 15th Regiment. While the regiment pushed on the objective by launching an amphibious assault, the Rangers moved inland by truck to San Angelo di Brolo and launched a similarly successful attack from the mountains. The Rangers' next target was Monteforte, which was taken with the aid of a detachment of pack howitzers transported by mules. By dawn on the 16th Darby was holding high ground above the town of Sanbruca, just four miles (6 km) west of Messina, and poised to move against the final Allied objective. The following day, once the Germans had completed their largely successful evacuation to mainland Italy, the Rangers marched into the coastal city, marking the end of the 38-day campaign.

Several Allied units were withdrawn from the Mediterranean theatre after the capture of Sicily to prepare for the D-Day landings in June 1944. Although Rangers were destined to play a key role during Operation Overlord, these were not part of Darby's command as both he and his men were earmarked for the forthcoming invasion and occupation of the Italian mainland. On August 18 Darby and his three battalions were gathered together and moved back across the island to Palermo to rest, receive replacements and prepare for their next task – the forthcoming assault on the Italian mainland. During their time at Palermo Darby's command was expanded to include a Ranger Cannon Company consisting of four half-track-mounted 75 mm guns under Shunstrom.

OPERATION AVALANCHE – THE SALERNO LANDINGS

On September 3 Montgomery's British Eighth Army launched Operation Baytown, crossing the Straits of Messina from Sicily and making unopposed landings at Reggio di Calabria on the very tip of the Italian mainland. Six days later, just hours before Italy announced an armistice, the Allies launched the two other prongs of their invasion of southern Italy. Operation Slapstick saw the British 1st Airborne Division put ashore from warships at the port of Taranto in the southeast, while General Mark Clark's US Fifth Army began Operation Avalanche, a larger assault against beaches in the Gulf of Salerno, some 45 miles (72 km) south of Naples on the west coast. Salerno was chosen in preference to a large-scale landing on the more distant Adriatic coast as Allied aircraft on Sicily could only guarantee cover over the former area, the nearby extensive port facilities at Naples were seen as a potentially valuable prize and it placed the Allies on the most direct route northwards to Rome.

The Rangers' role in Avalanche was to act as a flank guard to the main amphibious

Below: Operation Avalanche – the landings at Salerno on September 9, 1943 – saw the Rangers used as a flank guard for General Mark Clark's Fifth Army. The landings at Salerno were the largest amphibious operation of the war up to that date and were strongly resisted by the Germans. The counter-attacks of September 12–14 came close to pushing the Allies into the sea. It was only the weight of fire from offshore and the Allied air bombardment that enabled the beach-head to remain secure.

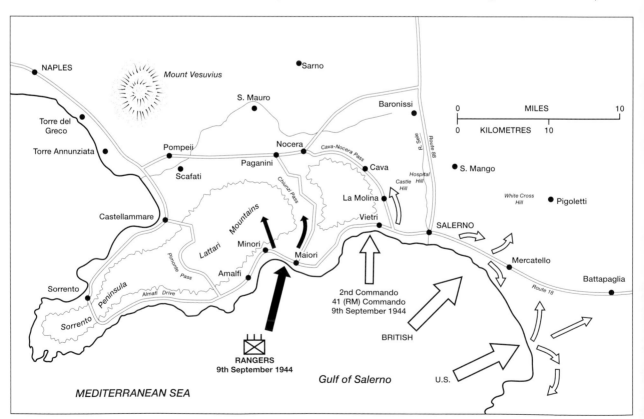

assaults of Clark's British X Corps and US VI Corps by securing the 25-mile (40 km) length of the Sorrento Peninsula and the Lattari Mountains, which divide the Gulfs of Naples and Salerno. Darby's command, which was temporarily attached to X Corps, was to land at a point some 10 miles (16 km) northwest of the more northerly of the two main landing sites and around seven miles (10 km) west of Salerno itself. Once ashore the various battalions were to push inland and establish blocking positions in the 3–4,000-foot (1,000 m) mountains to control the various passes through which any German reinforcements from the Naples area would have to travel to reach the main invasion beaches. The target area had three main passes – Cava–Nocera at the eastern, inland extremity of the peninsula, which was the most direct route from Naples to Salerno and though which Highway 18 snaked; the Chiunzi Pass some 5 miles (8 km) west of Cava–Nocera; and the Pimonte Pass, a tunnelled route that ran north-south to Castellammare on the southern shores of the Gulf of Naples. A fourth route, the Amalfi Drive, also circled around the peninsula's coastline by way of Sorrento and Castellammare and was another potential, if more circuitous, path for German troops heading for Salerno. The capture of the high ground would allow the Rangers to spot enemy troop movements in the surrounding lowlands and call down naval gunfire from Allied warships in the Gulf of Salerno on any potential targets by radio.

The Rangers were transported to a 1,000-yard-long (900 m) narrow stretch of beach around Maiori on the peninsula's southern coast in three Landing Ships Infantry (LSI) and five Landing Craft Infantry (LCI), guided to their objective by a British destroyer. Because of a shortage of landing craft – sufficient to land just one battalion at a time – the first assault wave was placed in the LCIs, while the follow-on units were shuttled to shore in the Landing Craft Assault carried by the LSIs. The 4th Rangers led the way, landing in the dead centre of the beach at around 0320 hours on September 9. Complete surprise had been achieved and the battalion quickly established blocking positions on either side of the beachhead and neutralized coastal defences in the vicinity of Capo d'Orso near Maiori, while the next waves, comprising the 1st and 3rd Rangers, were brought ashore in quick succession and then pushed rapidly inland towards the Chiunzi Pass.

Within three hours of landing the Rangers had accomplished their primary mission. Speed and surprise had enabled them quickly to overpower what limited opposition they encountered. By 0800 hours the 1st and 3rd Rangers were digging in on Monte St. Angelo di Cava and Monte di Chiunzi, 2,500–3,000-foot (900 m) heights on the eastern edge of the pass, while the accompanying 509th Parachute Infantry Battalion took up position on 4,000-foot (1,200 m) Monte Ceretto on the western edge of the pass. Daylight revealed that the Rangers indeed had panoramic views of the surrounding low ground, particularly the towns of Pagani and Nocera, and could easily bring down naval and artillery fire on any German forces heading for Salerno along Highway 18 or by rail through Nocera. As these units consolidated their positions, the 4th Battalion pushed westward along the Amalfi Drive and then moved northward through the Pimonte Pass to take Castellammare. The peninsula and its passes were effectively barred to the Germans by the 12th.

The German response to the Rangers' landing was swift. The 4th Battalion was soon pushed out of Castellammare and withdrew westward to Vico Equensa by way of the coastal Amalfi Drive. As they retreated the troops destroyed bridges and sections of raised roadway to slow their pursuers. The battalion held on to its positions around Vico Equensa for the next two weeks in the face of frequent German attacks but then withdrew along the coast road to the peninsula's south coast. New positions were established around Pimonte and the nearby route that ran directly northwards through the Pimonte Pass to Castellammare. The battalion faced German pressure on two fronts – from west to east

Above and next page: After Salerno, the Rangers fought effectively on the Italian Front – so much so that the 1st and 3rd Battalions received a Presidential Unit Citation (see box page 37). This sequence of photographs taken on November 10, 1943, shows Company D, 3rd Ranger Battalion, on patrol.

along the Amalfi Drive and from north to south through the Pimonte Pass – but the local terrain greatly aided its defence. The road in the pass ran through an 800-feet-long (250 m) tunnel and the Rangers dug in at its southern entrance and on the high ground either side. A 75 mm gun mounted on a half-track was sited on the tunnel's entrance and this, coupled with various other strongpoints, ensured that the Germans could not force their way through the pass. The Amalfi Drive, with the sea on one side and mountains on the other also provided ideal defensive terrain and, once again, the Germans were denied an alternative route to Salerno as the Rangers took up strong positions some two miles west of Amalfi.

Darby had expected his mission to last perhaps just a few days, certainly no more than a week, yet his Rangers had to remain in the hills for 21 days. The rapid breakout from Salerno by Clark's Fifth Army never materialized as the Germans fought stubbornly to throw the Allies back into the Mediterranean. As the pressure at Salerno mounted, it became even more imperative that the Rangers slow the flow of enemy reinforcements moving south from Naples. Thanks to excellent observation on the high ground overlooking Highway 18 and first-rate ship-to-shore communications, accurate gunfire from a British battleship, two cruisers and a shallow-draught monitor significantly reduced the flow of German reinforcements to the Salerno beaches. However, the Rangers had to contend with sometimes acute shortages of supplies, particularly food and ammunition, during their stay in the mountains and had to beat off numerous localized German counterattacks, while enduring frequent artillery and mortar bombardments.

The Allied breakout from Salerno finally began on the 20th. Clark's VI Corps first drove eastward in a looping attack toward Naples and, three days later, was joined by X Corps, which pushed directly northwards along Highway 18 towards the port. Able to observe this latter push, Darby ordered his men to strike for Pagani, close to Nocera at the northern end of the Chiunzi Pass, and also reoccupy Castellammare. With the Germans abandoning their positions in a staged withdrawal to the line of the Volturno River north of the port, the Rangers made steady progress by way of Pompeii and Mount Vesuvius in support of the US 82nd Airborne Division. Naples was liberated on October 1 and the Rangers moved in. Darby's casualties in the passes and subsequent advance totalled 13 killed and 21 seriously wounded in the 1st Battalion, seven killed, one missing and 14 wounded in the 3rd Battalion, and eight killed, eight missing and 21 wounded in the 4th Battalion. The 1st and 3rd Rangers received Presidential Unit Citations for their staunch defence of the Chiunzi Pass.

WINTER FIGHTING IN THE APPENNINES

The occupation of Naples proved to be no more than a brief respite for the Rangers. On October 3 they ended their attachment to X Corps and came under the direct command of the US Fifth Army. Just three days later Darby was ordered to prepare two of his battalions for renewed combat by the end of the month. By the 12th the Allied advance towards Rome had faltered along the Volturno River in an area some 40 miles (64 km) north of Naples that Kesselring had ordered defended to the utmost in order that he could prepare even stronger defences – the Gustav or Winter Line – along the Garigliano and Rapido Rivers. The Ranger battalions moved back south to the Sorrento Peninsula and established a camp at San Lazzaro, where they spent some two weeks resting, training and receiving replacements.

By the end of October the Allies had reached the Bernhard or Reinhard Line, an outer defensive zone covering the approaches to the Gustav Line that ran almost directly north–south across the central Italian mainland some 10 miles (16 km) east of Monte Cassino. It was here that the Rangers returned to combat. The 4th Battalion was the first to leave San Lazzaro and on November 1 joined the Fifth Army's US 3rd Division on the Volturno, where they helped secure a crossing over the river; the 1st Battalion left its base late on the 8th and completed the 30-mile (48 km) journey by truck to link up with the US 45th Division around Venafro at 0130 hours the following day. It was later joined by the 3rd Battalion, which was initially held back at San Lazzaro to integrate its larger body of replacements, and then both took part in fighting southwest of Venafro, serving successively with the US 45th and 36th Infantry Divisions.

The 1st Battalion immediately moved into position. Venafro, some 12 miles (20 km) due east of Cassino, was surrounded by commanding heights that provided excellent positions for spotting enemy troop movements. The Rangers occupied Monte Corno, supported by the 83rd Chemical Mortar Battalion and the Ranger Cannon Company, while the 509th Parachute Infantry Battalion took charge of the adjacent Monte San Croce. On the 11th the mortars and cannon company supported a successful attack by the paratroopers on the ridge that ran between the two peaks and gave them an uninterrupted view of the German-occupied village of Concacasalle. The 1st Rangers, joined by the 4th Battalion from the middle of the month, spent several weeks in the mountains. There were no major battles, but the Rangers conducted patrols and reconnaissance missions, and used their mortars to harass the Germans around Concacasalle. The weather was bitterly cold and the conditions, allied to frequent enemy shelling, ensured that the two Ranger units suffered a steady stream of casualties. The 3rd Battalion had also suffered during the fighting. It was tasked with leading the assault to take Monte Rotondo and the village of San Pietro on high ground along the eastern edge of the plain that leads to Cassino, but was stopped some 800 yards (700 m) outside the village. When this advance stalled, the battalion was transferred to Ceppagna close to Darby's other two units.

The Rangers' time around Venafro came to an end in mid-December. The 1st and 4th Battalions departed for Lucrino Station on Pozzuoli Bay to the west of Naples on the 14th, and the 3rd followed six days later. The various units were badly depleted, having suffered casualty rates of around 40 per cent during their time in the mountains due to the prolonged combat and the adverse weather. During the Christmas period they were allowed to relax and reorganize. Darby had recently been promoted to full colonel during a visit to Clark's headquarters at Caserta north of Naples and his various units were redesignated the 6615th Ranger Force (Provisional) on January 16, 1944. Aside from the 1st, 3rd and 4th Rangers, this formation included the 509th

PRESIDENTIAL UNIT CITATION
1ST AND 3RD RANGER BATTALIONS

The 1st and 3rd Ranger Battalions, with the following attached units:

319th Glider Field Artillery Battery;

Headquarters Battery, 80th Airborne Antiaircraft Battalion;

Battery D, 80th Airborne Antiaircraft Battalion;

Battery E, 80th Airborne Antiaircraft Battalion;

Battery F, 80th Airborne Antiaircraft Battalion;

Medical Detachment, 80th Airborne Antiaircraft Battalion;

Company H, 504th Parachute Infantry Regiment;

2nd Platoon, Company A, 307th Airborne Engineer Battalion,

are cited for outstanding performance of duty in action during the period 10th to 18th September 1943.

These units, comprising a single Ranger force, landed at Maiori, Italy, with the mission of seizing high ground controlling Chiunzi Pass and securing the left flank of the Fifth Army in its push northward into the plain of Naples. The position held by this force was vital not only for flank security, but also for observation of the plain and of the German supply routes and communications lines to the Salerno battlefront.

During this period, the Ranger force was subjected to almost continuous mortar and artillery fire and was repeatedly attacked by a determined enemy. Hostile forces were estimated to outnumber the Rangers and attached units by approximately eight to one, but despite superior enemy numbers, the Ranger force heroically fought off every attempt to dislodge it.

Because of its limited strength and the large area assigned to it for defense, the force held the line thinly, marked with strongpoints with gaps covered by fire.

Several major counterattacks were repelled during the period and numerous enemy patrols were stopped, often in bitter, close-in fighting, with the Ranger force using its mortars, artillery, automatic weapons, and grenades with devastating effect.

The officers and men of these units fought without rest or relief and with limited food and water supplies. The continuous nature of the enemy fire and activity was such as to try the men to the limits of their endurance.

Although overwhelming enemy forces drove almost constantly at the sparsely held positions, the determination and courage of the 1st and 3rd Ranger Battalions and their attached units offset the enemy superiority in numbers and made possible the successful accomplishment of a vital mission.

Official: Dwight D. Eisenhower
Edward F. Witsel   Chief of Staff
Major-General
The Adjutant General

Above: Italy, January 1, 1944 – 80 men of 1st Ranger Battalion line up to receive decorations from Brigadier-General Theodore Roosevelt.

The Anzio landings, part of a plan to force the Gustav Line, took place on January 22, 1944. Training for them involved three weeks of amphibious practices and physical exercise.

Right: January 14, 1944. Men of 2nd Platoon, Company A, 1st Rangers do their usual log exercises.

Above right: January 16, 1944. Soldiers of 3rd Ranger Battalion photographed at Baia in front of the landing craft that will take them to the Anzio landings. By the 29th all but six of the 767 men from the 1st and 3rd Battalions were either dead or prisoners.

Far right: January 14, 1944. 1st Rangers load into British LCAs for beach-landing manoeuvres near Naples.

Above: November 10, 1943: a medic treats a leg wound sustained during a skirmish by Pfc John Brady of the 3rd Ranger Battalion.

Above right: Operation Shingle – the landings at Anzio by US and British forces under the command of General Lucas. This map shows the Rangers' part in the battle.

Below right: 1st Ranger Battalion troops board vessels at Baia.

Parachute Infantry Battalion, the 83rd Chemical Mortar Battalion, Company H, 36th Engineer Regiment, and the half-track-mounted Ranger Cannon Company. The regrouping was a prelude to what was to be Darby's fourth and final amphibious assault – Operation Shingle, the landings by the Anglo-US VI Corps under Major General John Lucas at Anzio some 40 miles (64 km) south of Rome, which were supposed to break the stalemate at Cassino by establishing a threatening beachhead behind the German lines and forcing them to retreat northwards.

ANZIO – THE RANGERS' NEMESIS

After some three weeks of vital amphibious training for the new recruits arriving at Pozzuoli, the Rangers boarded their assault vessels anchored off Baia on January 20 in preparation for the 120-mile (190 km) voyage northwards to Anzio. The transports comprised *Princess Beatrix*, *Winchester Castle*, a pair of landing craft, tank, a single landing ship, tank, and HMS *Royal Ulsterman*, which had seen service with the Rangers during the Arzew landings and whose presence was seen as a favourable omen. The Anzio operation opened early on January 22, with the Rangers undertaking the spearhead role by landing on beaches at Anzio itself. The 1st and 4th Rangers came ashore first, beginning at 0200 hours, and quickly fanned out through Anzio with some making for Nettuno to the east. Opposition was extremely light and the engineers accompanying Darby's command set about clearing beach obstacles and mines, while landing craft returned with the 3rd Battalion. The port was secured by 0800 hours and throughout the day the Rangers extended their perimeter by linking up with the British 1st Infantry Division at Peter Beach to the north of Anzio and the US 3rd Infantry Division at X-Ray Beach around Nettuno.

For the next two days, the beachhead expanded slowly as more and more Allied troops poured ashore. The Rangers held the central sector of the perimeter, a flat area bisected by drainage ditches and dotted with woodland between one road running due north from Anzio to Carroceto and another from Nettuno to Padiglione. It quickly became apparent that the Germans, who were rushing reinforcements into the area while Lucas failed to capitalize on the element of surprise, held the high ground overlooking the Allied positions and could rain down artillery fire on the Anzio plain at will. The Rangers initially engaged in patrol work but for the most part kept to their foxholes. However, on the 25th Darby was ordered to support an advance by the British 1st Division towards Carroceto. The 4th Battalion led the way, having to negotiate numerous drainage ditches, while the remaining two battalions initially remained in reserve. Support was provided by a US paratrooper battalion and a detachment of tank destroyers. While the British faced stubborn resistance at Carroceto, the Rangers had to deal with snipers, enemy mortar fire, and frequent firefights. However, the subsidiary role at Carroceto was only a prelude to a much more ambitious operation to break out of the beachhead.

By late January Lucas, who was under increasing pressure from his superiors to act decisively, felt compelled to launch a major breakout from Anzio. This called for a simultaneous two-pronged effort on the night of the 28th, one by British forces in the direction of Campoleone from Carroceto and the second to the east by the US 3rd Division. The Rangers, supported by the US 504th Parachute Infantry Regiment, were tasked with leading the 3rd Division's attack, which was directed towards the town of Cisterna. The plan was for the Rangers to advance under cover of darkness some four miles (6 km) beyond the northeast sector of the existing Allied perimeter, capture Cisterna and then hold it for a few hours until larger forces arrived on the scene. Cisterna was of considerable importance to the ongoing Italian campaign as it was a hub of communications running southeast from Rome to Monte Cassino. In German hands

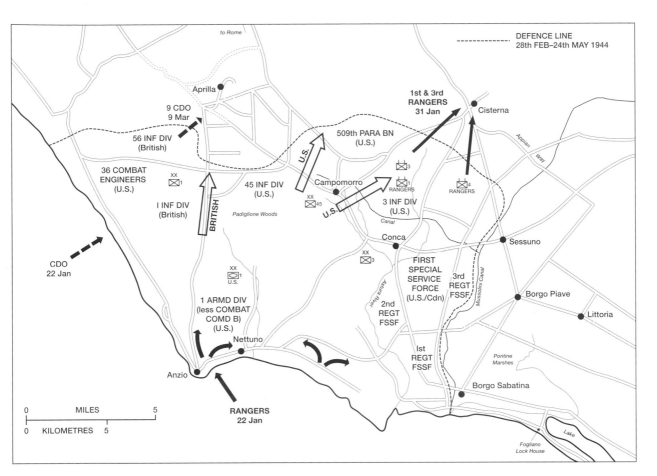

DEFENCE LINE
28th FEB–24th MAY 1944

to Rome

Aprilla

9 CDO
9 Mar

56 INF DIV
(British)

1st & 3rd
RANGERS
31 Jan

Cisterna

509th PARA BN
(U.S.)

36 COMBAT
ENGINEERS
(U.S.)

XX
1

U.S.

Campomorro

XX
3

XX
1
RANGERS

XX
4
RANGERS

Appian Way

I INF DIV
(British)

45 INF DIV
(U.S.)

XX
45

3 INF DIV
(U.S.)

BRITISH

Padiglione Woods

Canal

U.S.

Conca

Sessuno

XX
1
U.S.

XX
3

FIRST
SPECIAL
SERVICE
FORCE
(U.S./Cdn)

3rd
REGT
FSSF

CDO
22 Jan

1 ARMD DIV
(less COMBAT
COMD B)
(U.S.)

Nettuno

Astura River

2nd
REGT
FSSF

Mussolini Canal

Borgo Piave

Littoria

Anzio

RANGERS
22 Jan

1st
REGT
FSSF

Pontine
Marshes

Borgo Sabatina

0   MILES   5
0   KILOMETRES   5

Fogliano
Lock House

Lake

Highway 7 and the railway that ran through Cisterna were used to ferry troops to the Gustav Line; if the town was in Allied hands then the severing of these two arteries might lead to a German withdrawal from Cassino and facilitate a rapid drive on the Italian capital.

The plan was for the Rangers to crawl forward from the existing front line in virtual single file along a ditch, the Fossa di Pantano, which was an offshoot of the western branch of the Mussolini Canal and ended just two miles (3 km) short of Cisterna. They would then debouch onto the open land outside the town and follow the line of the road running between it and Nettuno by way of the village of Isola Bella to their objective. It was a tricky plan, but one that the Rangers were trained for and experienced enough to accomplish, and intelligence indicated that the local opposition was expected to be light. However, events conspired against the Rangers even before they opened their attack. Returning from a planning meeting shortly before commencing their unit's spearhead attack against Campoleone, several British officers took a wrong turning and were killed in a German ambush. Consequently a new unit had to be assigned the task and its officers briefed on what was expected of them. This inevitably caused a delay and the twin-pronged offensive did not open until the night of the 29th – some 24 hours later than intended. In the interim the Germans had moved forces into the area of Cisterna in preparation for launching a major counterattack on the Anzio beachhead. Rather than facing just elements of the *Hermann Göring* Division, the Rangers were now also confronted by units from the 26th Panzergrenadier and 715th Infantry Divisions.

Unaware of these developments, the Rangers opened the advance on Cisterna late on the 29th. The advance was led by the 1st and 3rd Battalions, which had infiltrated between the opposing front lines, seemingly without being spotted, by 0100 hours on the 30th. The 4th Battalion and the Ranger Cannon Company, tasked with clearing the Anzio–Cisterna road for follow-on forces, moved off at 0200 hours but had advanced just 800 yards (700 m) before being hit by heavy enemy fire. As dawn broke the difficulty of the situation became evident – the leading two battalions were well short of Cisterna and were fighting in isolated companies and platoons against a much stronger enemy force. Worse, the 4th Rangers was first delayed by heavy fighting at Isola Bella and then brought to a complete halt at Femina Morta well short of the other battalions. News also reached Darby that the commander of the 3rd Battalion, Major Alvah Miller, had been killed by a shell fired by a tank.

The Rangers' predicament became clearer at around 0830 hours. The 1st Battalion's commander, Major Jack Dobson, radioed that he was surrounded some 800 yards short of Cisterna and that German fire was causing heavy losses among his troops in their open positions. The 3rd Battalion was in a similar situation. The 4th Battalion and units of the US 3rd Infantry Division struggled to relieve the trapped Rangers but were unable to break through. By early afternoon, the 1st and 3rd Battalions – what remained of them – were at the end of their tether. Some Rangers fought on until killed, others, many of them wounded, surrendered, and a handful withdrew to friendly lines. The 4th

Above: A German casualty lies next to his Kübelwagen, Anzio.

Right and Below right: As a footnote to Anzio, these two photographs, taken June 21, 1944, show a guerrilla band formed of escapees from a German prison train. A number of these men were Rangers who had been captured during the attack on Cisterna. They escaped and operated behind enemy lines disrupting enemy communications before reaching their own forces.

Below: Burying the dead during the Italian campaign.

Battalion itself was effectively surrounded but held on until relieved on the morning of the 31st. Supported by other troops it finally captured Femina Morta, but this was a trifle compared to the virtual annihilation of the 1st and 3rd Battalions.

The crushing reverse at Cisterna effectively wiped the three Ranger battalions from the US order of battle in Europe. Only six of 767 men from the 1st and 3rd Battalions managed to escape from the killing fields outside the town; the remainder were either dead or prisoners. Some 500 captured Rangers were paraded through central Rome by the Germans, an event recorded on film for propaganda purposes. After the battle the 4th Battalion was in little better shape but still saw further action at Anzio, chiefly in helping to blunt a counterattack against the beachhead perimeter in early February, and then, following the breakout and liberation of Rome in late May and early June, it operated at the Fifth Army's patrolling school at Civitavecchia to the north of the Italian capital. The remnants of the 1st and 3rd Battalions, the handful who had survived Cisterna and support personnel who had not taken part in the fighting – about 150 in total – had already been withdrawn and sent to Camp Butner, North Carolina, in early May. Some became instructors at infantry training schools, while others were reassigned to the US-Canadian 1st Special Service Force's 1st Regiment. The 1st and 3rd Battalions were officially deactivated on August 15 and the 4th followed on October 26.

RAIDING OCCUPIED EUROPE

While Darby's battalion was fighting in North Africa, a short-lived Ranger unit was activated back in England to conduct pinprick raids along the coast of occupied Europe. In September 1942, with the departure of Darby's unit for North Africa imminent, plans were laid for the creation of a new Ranger battalion from US personnel stationed in Britain. On December 20 the 29th Provisional Ranger Battalion came into existence at Tidworth Barracks in Wiltshire and was commanded by Major Randolph Millholland.

Below: It wasn't only in Britain that Rangers were being selected and trained. This photograph (and that opposite) are of Fort Jackson, South Carolina, on April 22, 1943, as Ranger recruits undergoe live fire training. Established on June 2, 1917, the new Army Training Center was named in honour of Major General Andrew Jackson, the seventh president of the United States. The first military unit to be organized here was the 81st 'Wildcat' Division. In 1939 Fort Jackson was organized as an infantry training centre. Four firing ranges were constructed, and more than 500,000 men received some phase of their training here. Today the camp is the largest and most active Initial Entry Training Center in the United States Army, providing training to almost 50 percent of the men and women who enter the service each year.

Officers and men were volunteers drawn from the US 29th Infantry Division and 18 members of the 1st Battalion were detached to train the new recruits. As with previous Ranger units, the 29th moved to Achnacarry for Commando training and then on to Spean Bridge to learn amphibious assault techniques. The programme was completed by February 1943 and the Rangers moved to Dartmouth where they were attached to No. 14 Commando for the following six weeks.

Unlike other Ranger units, the 29th Battalion conducted hazardous small-scale raids, usually involving one or two men accompanied by British Commandos. These were nuisance missions against Occupied Europe, chiefly along the coast of Norway and northern France, and were not always successful. One of three such raids against Norway involving the 29th Battalion, code named Roundabout, took place on March 23, when five Rangers, three British and five Norwegian Commandos came ashore at Landet with the intention of attacking enemy shipping. However, the mission ended prematurely when the raiders were discovered by German sentries. In May the battalion moved to Bude, Cornwall, and then to HMS *Dorlin* during July. The 29th Rangers' last operation was code named Pound. A party of 18 men from No. 12 Commando and two Rangers landed on the island of Ushant off the west coast of Brittany during the night of September 3–4 to attack a German radar station. A German sentry (possibly two) was killed and then the raiders returned home unscathed. Pound was the unit's last action due to the imminent arrival of the 2nd and 5th Rangers from the United States and the scaling down of British Commando raids across the Channel. After the Ushant raid the battalion spent time at Dover but was deactivated while based at Okehampton, Devon, on October 15 and its personnel returned to the 29th Division.

The Rangers practised opposed landings from the sea from the earliest days in Scotland in August 1942 – as these photos show. Still wearing their British-style M1917A1 helmets, the men of 1st Rangers practise on a cold Scottish loch the skills that were to prove so effective in Normandy less than two years later. By the time of the Normandy landings, the Allies in general and their special forces – Rangers, Commandos, etc – in particular had a great deal of practical experience in amphibious warfare and landing on defended coasts. On top of this, they had specialist equipment – especially all forms of landing craft – that gave them the technological edge.

14099

PREPARING FOR OPERATION OVERLORD

The brief service of the 29th Provisional Battalion in 1942 and the deactivation of the 1st, 3rd and 4th Battalions in 1944 did not signal the end of the Rangers' involvement in World War II. On March 11, 1943, while Darby's 1st Battalion was fighting in Tunisia, a directive had been issued to form a 2nd Battalion, which was activated at Camp Forrest, Tennessee, under the command of Lieutenant Colonel William Saffarans on April 1. Some 2,000 volunteers were evaluated and about 500 accepted for training under the watchful eyes of ex-1st Battalion officers and non-commissioned officers. Saffarans and three other commanders came and went, but in June Major James Rudder took command, and the battalion commenced specialist training. In September, its men went through the Scouts' and Raiders' School at Fort Pierce, Florida, where they learned to work with small assault craft and boats. Next the battalion moved to Fort Dix, New Jersey, to practise advanced tactical techniques. Deemed ready for active service, the battalion sailed for England on the liner *Queen Elizabeth* on November 21.

The 2nd Rangers was soon joined by a further battalion as US planners felt that two such specialist units would be needed for the invasion of Occupied Europe. The 5th Battalion was activated at Camp Forrest on September 1 and in November followed the 2nd Battalion through Fort Pierce and then, from the 20th, trained at Fort Dix. It sailed for England in January 1944.

Main photograph: Live fire opposed landing exercise in Scotland, August 1942.

Inset, Left and Right: Wire was a major obstacle on defended beaches. Bangalore torpedoes were the chief anti-wire weapon. Photos are of 29th Battalion.

Meanwhile, once in England, the 2nd Battalion was initially stationed at Bude, north Cornwall, and continued to concentrate on training, although individual Rangers served with British Commando parties during several small cross-Channel raids. Many of these were designed to gain intelligence or as nuisance raids to mislead the Germans as to where the Allied invasion would take place. On the night of December 26–27, 1943, for example, two Rangers took part in Operation Hardtack 4, which was designed to assess the beach defences at Ault, south of the Somme Estuary and some distance from the Normandy area. On the 28th the battalion moved to Titchfield Barracks and subsequently underwent cliff-assault training in the Isle of Wight: It returned to Bude in February 1944 and in April spent some weeks at the Assault Training Centre at Woolacombe in north Devon before moving to Dorchester in Dorset on the 27th.

The 5th Battalion under Major Max Schneider arrived at Liverpool on January 18 and was initially based at Leominster before spending time at the Commando Training Depot at Achnacarry in March and the Assault Training Centre in April. Further periods of training followed, but on May 5 the two battalions were united at Dorchester and a day later Rudder was placed in command of what was named the Provisional Ranger Group. By the end of the month the battalions had moved to their final marshalling area around Swanage for embarkation in preparation for their spearhead role on D-Day.

Left: Practice night landing, January 1944.

Right and Below: It could almost be Normandy – the pill boxes and gullies of Omaha, and the cliffs of Pointe du Hoc. In fact the photos are taken on the north coast of Devon, England, around Bude. The wide expanse of sand, with dunes and some cliffs provided the Rangers and other Allied forces with the perfect place to hone their landing techniques . . . and, of course, maintain their physical fitness thanks to the ubiquitous pole routine.

Right: The attack on Pointe du Hoc – a brave and brilliantly executed special force attack in no way belittled by the fact that the Germans had not positioned their guns in the casemates.

LEONARD LOMELL

Lomell was a first sergeant with Company D, 2nd Rangers, and, although wounded in the initial landings at the base of the Pointe du Hoc on D-Day, he scaled the cliffs and played a key role in the mission, winning the Distinguished Service Cross for the destruction of three 155 mm guns:

'... Jack Kuhn [also to win the DSC] and I went down this sunken road not knowing where the hell it was going, but it was going inland. We came upon this vale or little draw with camouflage all over it, and lo and behold, we peeked over this hedgerow, and there were the guns. It was pure luck. They were all sitting in proper firing condition, with ammunition piled up neatly, everything at the ready, but they were pointed at Utah Beach, not Omaha. There was nobody at the emplacement. We looked round cautiously, and over about 100 yards away in a corner of a field was a vehicle with what looked like an officer talking to his men.

We decided that nobody was here so let's take a chance. I said; "Jack, you cover me and I'm going in there and destroy them." So all I had was two thermite grenades – his and mine. I went in and put the thermite grenades in the traversing mechanism, and that knocked out two of them because that melted their gears in a moment. And then I broke their sights, and we ran back to the road, which was 100 yards or so back, and got all the other thermites from the remainder of my guys manning the roadblock, and rushed back and put the grenades in traversing mechanisms, elevation mechanisms, and banged the sights. There was no noise to that. There is no noise to a thermite, so no one saw us...'

ASSAULTING THE POINTE DU HOC

The Ranger Group was attached to the US 29th Infantry Division's 116th Regiment for Operation Overlord and was detailed to undertake one of the the most hazardous missions conducted on D-Day. Omaha Beach was overlooked by the commanding cliffs of the Pointe du Hoc to the west and intelligence had identified a six-gun German coastal battery being installed on the cliff-top that could sweep the beach and target any invasion fleet. The garrison was estimated at 200 men from the 716th Coastal Defence Division.

The Pointe du Hoc assault opened at 0540 hours on June 6, 1944, with a bombardment of the cliff-top from the battleship USS *Texas*, which was followed by an attack from 19 A-20 Boston medium bombers from the US Ninth Air Force. Those Rangers earmarked to lead the attack, 225 men from Companies D, E, F of the 2nd Battalion under the direct command of Lieutenant Colonel Rudder, had a difficult approach. They boarded their Landing Craft, Assault (LCAs) from two transports, *Amsterdam* and *Ben-my-Chree*, amid rough seas. It was expected that the journey to shore would take around three hours but the LCAs were buffeted by high waves and the troops and crews were quickly drenched or convulsed by seasickness. Two of the three accompanying heavily laden supply craft sank. Worse, one of the landing craft, *LCA.860*, with 20 Rangers from Company D aboard was also lost, although the men were rescued by a motor launch and returned to England. Finally, a navigation error by the commander of the leading LCA, that with Rudder on board, led the flotilla towards another promontory, Pointe de la Percée, three miles (5 km) to the east of the objective. Rudder spotted the error but the course correction delayed the attack for some 40 minutes. This had far-reaching repercussions. First the slow-moving LCAs had to sail westwards parallel to the coast and only 100 yards (100 m) or so offshore to reach the Pointe du Hoc, and in doing so came under close-range enemy fire. Second, the naval bombardment by the *Texas* ended exactly on schedule as it was believed that the Rangers had landed successfully and on time. The loss of fire support allowed the defenders to emerge from their bunkers and man their positions. Two destroyers, the USS *Satterlee* and HMS *Talybont*, used their main armament to rectify the situation but their weight of shell was obviously much less than that of the battleship. Finally, the remainder of the 2nd Battalion and the whole of Schneider's 5th Rangers were supposed to land in direct support of Rudder when the latter fired flares to signals to signify a successful landing. Because of the delay no flares were seen at the expected time and at 0700 Schneider adopted the pre-agreed alternative plan. The codeword Tilt was issued and the LCAs carrying a battalion and a half of Rangers swung away from the Pointe du Hoc and made for the western end of Omaha Beach.

Rudder's three companies, which had lost 40 men during the approach, landed on the narrow beach below the cliff and quickly discovered that their problems were far from over. Aside from the alert defenders, much of their specialist climbing equipment was unusable. The DUKWs with turntable ladders were unable to cross the crater-pocked landing site, and many of the rocket-propelled grapnels for their climbing ropes were useless as the saturated ropes were far too heavy to be fired to the top of the cliff. Nevertheless the attack continued; some grapnels were still operable and the Rangers had their sectional ladders to hand. Others simply resorted to climbing the cliff by hand, seeking out footholds in the cliff face. Despite intense German fire and the severing of several ropes that pitched Rangers to their deaths, Rudder's men inched their way upwards. At 0730 the commander received a radio message, 'Praise the Lord,' indicating that some of his men had reached the summit and were fighting inland towards the coastal road running between Grandcamp-les-Bains to the west and Vierville-sur-Mer to

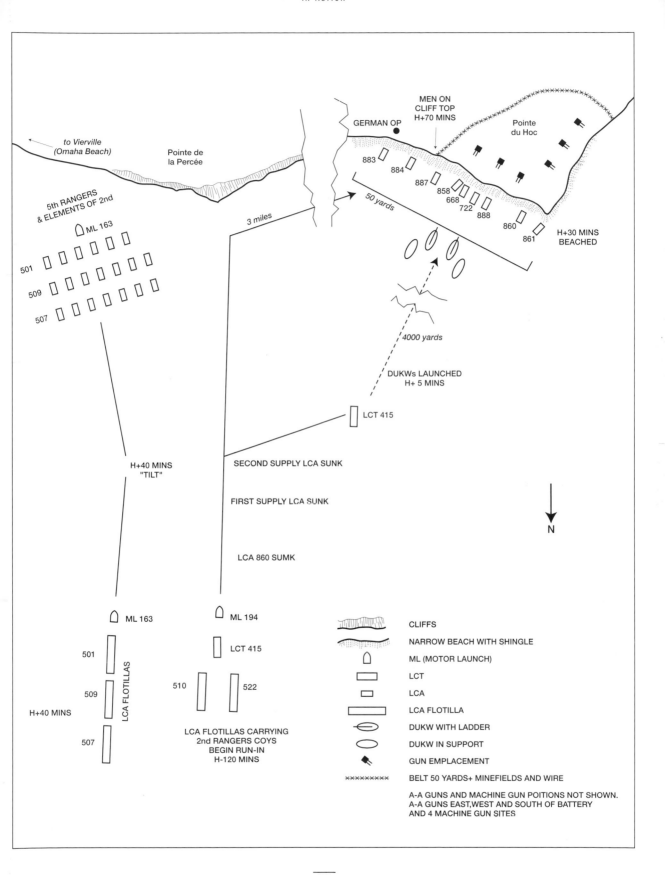

Above: It would be only on D+2 that relief came and prisoners could be taken away. Note the Stars and Stripes prominently displayed. This was to stop friendly fire problems – some Rangers were lost to Allied tank fire on D+1.

Left: Aerial view of Pointe du Hoc. Heavily bombarded by Allied aircraft in the days preceding D-Day, and by the battleship *Texas*, nevertheless the position was difficult to assault, thanks to the 100 ft (30 m) cliffs and a tenacious defence. It was even more difficult to hold: short of men (Rudder was down to 70 effectives) the Rangers performed heroics in the face of German counter-attacks.

Far left: The way up the Pointe – photograph taken D+2 when the way up was being used for supplies. Note the joined toggle rope. Compare this photograph with those of the re-enactment on pages 66 onwards.

Above: US troops land on Omaha Beach: the scene of the worst casualties on D-Day – over 2,000. The 5th Rangers and three companies of the 3rd (the other three were attacking Pointe du Hoc) landed on the west of Omaha.

the east. Reports also indicated that resistance was less than expected, chiefly because the naval and air bombardments had not only turned the Pointe du Hoc into a shell-cratered wasteland but had also dazed and demoralized many of the defenders. The Rangers now sought out the coastal guns but only discovered their emplacements. The mystery was solved at around 0900 when the guns were discovered about 880 yards inland, hidden under camouflage and waiting to be installed in their final positions. While these guns were destroyed, Rudder sent a message to his superiors shortly after midday: 'Located Pointe du Hoe [*sic*]. Mission accomplished. Need ammunition and reinforcements. Many casualties.' It was no more than the truth; his command, split into small groups with an estimated effective strength of 100 men, was facing severe German counterattacks, and the supply situation was critical as much-needed ammunition had been lost on the sunk supply craft.

If Rudder's men were not to be overwhelmed, it was essential that the 5th Rangers fight their way off Omaha Beach and head westwards for the Pointe du Hoc, but Schneider's men, like all the US forces committed to Omaha, were facing a difficult task. Their landing was well executed and there were few casualties but the men had to seek shelter behind a low sea wall to avoid murderous enemy fire. With the landings on Omaha in clear jeopardy, the assistant commander of the 29th Division, General Norman Cota, turned to Schneider's men at around 1000. Fearing his troops would never get off the beach, he issued a terse order: 'Lead the way, Rangers.' Individual platoons now began to move forward and seek a way inland between minefields and various other obstacles and were eventually able to reach a road running parallel to the coast some 1,000 yards (900 m) inland and leading to Vierville, which lay on the western edge of Omaha and blocked the direct route to the Pointe du Hoc. By nightfall, the bulk of the 5th Battalion was holding the western fringe of Vierville but was still short of its objective, although a platoon from Company A was able to swing south of the town and reach Rudder. During the 7th Rudder's men beat off several counterattacks, partly aided by naval support, received some much-needed supplies and had their strength boosted by a second platoon from the 5th Rangers. At 1700 hours that afternoon he was ordered to strike out towards Vierville to link up with a relief column comprising Companies A, B, and C of the 2nd Rangers, the whole of the remaining 5th Rangers and 150 men from the 116th RCT. Despite having tanks in support, this force was halted by artillery fire near St. Pierre-de-Mont, forcing Rudder to hold out for a second night. A second relief attempt was mounted on the morning of the 8th. The 5th Rangers and two battalions from the 116th Infantry pushed forward from around St. Pierre-de-Mont and finally reached Rudder's perimeter, thereby ending the battle for the Pointe du Hoc. Both battalions subsequently moved into Grandcamp. The action had cost Rudder 135 casualties but earned his unit a Presidential Unit Citation, an honour also granted to the 5th Battalion. Over the following days both battalions helped in the capture of Grandcamp and dealt with pockets of German resistance around Grandcamp and Isigny.

FROM NORMANDY TO VICTORY

After a spell integrating replacements and providing security details during June and July, the 2nd and 5th Battalions' next major role was to exploit the Allied breakout of the Normandy bridgehead that followed the success of Operation Cobra in late July. Once Patton's Third Army had successfully funnelled through the bottlenecks at Avranches and Pontaubault that led from southwest Normandy into northeast Brittany, it then spread out on a wide front, with two corps detailed to seize Brittany and the numerous ports defended by the German XXV Corps. Moving on a narrow front Major General Troy Middleton's US VIII Corps struck westwards towards Brest along the peninsula's north coast and southwest towards Rennes, while Major General Walton Walker's US XX Corps headed due south to St. Nazaire to seal off Brittany from the rest of France.

The US forces pushed forward quickly, with the US 6th Armored Division making rapid progress towards Brest. The division, which had moved through Pontaubault on August 2, reached the port four days later but failed to force the garrison, 30,000 troops of the German II Parachute Corps under General Hermann Ramcke, to surrender. The heavily defended port had to be taken by a formal siege, carried out by the US 2nd, 8th and 29th Infantry Divisions, Allied aircraft and warships, French Resistance units and the two Ranger battalions. Operations only commenced on August 25, being delayed because of the need to capture St. Mâlo. Brest was ringed by around 75 major concrete emplacements and these had to be taken one by one often using flamethrowers, satchel charges and shaped charges to pierce their armour. The Rangers were flung into the battle to neutralize several key defences. It took Rudder's 2nd Battalion several days of hard fighting between September 5 and 9 to seize the Lochrist battery but the Rangers eventually captured some 1,800 prisoners. The 5th Battalion helped capture Le Conquet after a two-hour fight and stormed La Mon Blanche with less difficulty, but its attack on Fort de Portzic, which opened on the 17th, lasted for two days, though its fall signalled the end of German resistance. Brest, the town and its harbour facilities in ruins, surrendered on the 18th.

After Brittany both battalions moved eastwards, participating in the Allied drive towards the German border and performing a number of functions. The 5th Battalion acted as a headquarters security force for General Omar Bradley's Twelfth Army Group in Belgium during October and November. In December it linked up with the US 6th Cavalry Group of Patton's Third Army and conducted various small-scale actions against enemy-held towns. After a spell attached to the US 95th Infantry Division in January 1945, the battalion joined the 94th Infantry Division on February 9, taking over a large section of the front near Wehingen.

It was during this period that the 5th Rangers undertook an operation more suited to its skills. On February 23, the unit pushed out from the bridgehead over the Saar River and fought its way to a point three miles (5 km) behind German lines to seize high

THE RANGER CREED

Recognizing that I volunteered as a Ranger, fully knowing the hazards of my chosen profession, I will always endeavor to uphold the prestige, honor, and esprit de corps of my Ranger Regiment.

Acknowledging the fact that a Ranger is a more elite soldier who arrives at the cutting edge of battle by land, sea, or air, I accept the fact that as a Ranger my country expects me to move farther, faster and fight harder than any other soldier.

Never shall I fail my comrades. I will always keep myself mentally alert, physically strong and morally straight and I will shoulder more than my fair share of the task whatever it may be. One hundred percent and then some.

Gallantly will I show the world that I am a specially selected and well-trained soldier. My courtesy to superior officers, neatness of dress and care of equipment shall set an example for others to follow.

Energetically will I meet the enemies of my country. I shall defeat them on the field of battle for I am better trained and will fight with all my might. Surrender is not a Ranger word. I will never leave a fallen comrade to fall into the hands of the enemy and under no circumstances will I ever embarrass my country.

Readily will I display the intestinal fortitude required to fight on to the Ranger objective and complete the mission though I be the lone survivor.

Right: Company C, 2nd Ranger Battalion, prepares for a patrol. Note the variety of equipment – all wear the M1941 field jacket but with various bits of webbing and different footwear. The man in the centre rests his BAR on the ground.

Below right: 6th Rangers in the first wave attacking Dinagat, October 17, 1944.

Below: The patrol goes out near Heimbach, Germany, March 3, 1945.

ground overlooking the supply road linking Irsch and Zerf two days later. Isolated and outnumbered, the battalion fought on alone until relieved by elements of the US 10th Armored Division on the afternoon of the 27th. Holding the roadblock cost the battalion around 90 casualties but it killed an estimated 300 German troops, wounded 500 and took another 300 prisoner, earning a Presidential Unit Citation for the action. The fighting aided the drive of armour towards Trier, allowing elements of the US XX Corps to reach the River Rhine.

The 5th Rangers spent March in Luxembourg integrating replacements for the losses suffered during the Irsch–Zerf action but then conducted security roles, such as guarding prisoners and overseeing affairs in liberated towns. In May, in one of the battalion's last actions, it served with the US 3rd Cavalry Group in the drive on Austria through southern Germany and secured largely undefended bridges over the Danube River.

The 2nd Battalion also moved eastwards after the fall of Brest, advancing through Belgium and then undertaking a period of training in Luxembourg during October. Returning to combat, the Rangers were attached to the US 28th Infantry Division and took part in the battle to clear the Hürtgen Forest. In December Rudder was promoted and transferred to take command of the US 109th Infantry Regiment, part of the US 28th Infantry Division, and Major George Williams took charge of the 2nd Battalion, which operated in a defensive role during the German Ardennes offensive. In January 1945 the weakened battalion was pulled out of the line and set up camp at Schnidthof in Germany, where replacements were integrated into the unit. In February the battalion served with the US 102nd Cavalry Group and participated in the crossing of the Roer River during March. April saw the battalion performing security details.

Germany's surrender heralded the demise of the two battalions. In May, following the completion of various internal security duties, the 2nd Rangers established a base at Dolreuth in Czechoslovakia, where it was reduced to zero strength in June and formally deactivated at Camp Patrick Henry, Virginia, on October 23. The same fate befell the 5th Battalion. Based at Ried, Austria, in May and June, it was reduced to zero strength and formally deactivated on October 22 at Camp Miles Standish, Massachusetts. The end of the two battalions did not, however, signal the end of Ranger participation in World War II.

RANGERS IN THE PACIFIC

Although the bulk of the Ranger battalions served in the European theatre, the need for a similar force to operate against the Japanese in the Pacific was recognized by the commander of the US Sixth Army, Lieutenant General Walter Krueger, in the penultimate year of the war. In spring 1944, with the invasion and liberation of the Philippines becoming a real possibility, a lieutenant colonel and former provost marshal of Honolulu, Henry A. Mucci, took charge of the 98th Field Artillery Battalion, which had seen action on New Georgia and was earmarked for conversion. The unit soon lost its 75 mm howitzers, while those men not wishing to convert to Rangers were transferred out and replacements integrated into the new structure. As the necessary intensive training programme continued near Port Moresby, the 6th Ranger Battalion was officially activated at Hollandia, Dutch East Indies, on September 24, 1944.

The 6th Rangers went into action a few weeks later as part of the preliminary stages of the invasion of Leyte and thereby become the first US troops to return to the Philippines since the Japanese occupation in 1942. The battalion's mission was to neutralize radio and radar stations on three islands that covered the main route to the landing beaches on Leyte. They were also to set up navigation lights to guide the main invasion fleet to its ultimate target. On October 17, 1944, three days before the main

Above: Company E, 6th Rangers, board assault craft October 17, 1944.

Opposite, above: Men of Companies B and E, 6th Rangers, going ashore behind an armoured bulldozer, Santiago Island, Luzon, January 20, 1945.

Opposite, below left: Guerrillas meet up with Rangers on Dinagat Island, October 18, 1944.

Opposite, below right: Raising the Stars and Stripes on Dinagat.

assault, part of the battalion's headquarters company and its Company D came ashore on Suluan Island, while most of the remainder of the unit landed on the larger island of Dinagat. At Dinagat, the Rangers disembarked from their five Auxiliary Personnel Destroyers into landing craft and began their run to shore at around 0930. Despite problems caused by reefs, all of the assault companies were ashore on the island's northwest coast by 1230 and patrols were searching for the small enemy garrison. While the sweeps of Suluan and Dinagat continued, the rest of the headquarters company and Company B assaulted Homonhon Island during the following day. The detachments on Suluan and Homonhon quickly achieved their objectives and then headed to Dinagat, the largest of the three islands, to link up with the main party. For the next few weeks the battalion conducted patrols out of the coastal village of Loreto, observing Japanese ship movements and air attacks, and mopping up isolated pockets of resistance, but on November 14 the Rangers sailed for Leyte.

The 6th Battalion fought on Leyte for several weeks and fulfilled several roles. In the second half of November and December, the Rangers acted as guards for the Sixth Army headquarters at Tanuan and Tolosa and also protected a Seebee construction unit building an airfield at the former location. They next participated in the invasion of Luzon, the main island of the Philippines. Landings at Lingayen Gulf by Krueger's Sixth Army began on January 9, 1945, but the Rangers did not spearhead the assault and came ashore during the 10th and 11th. For the next few weeks the battalion acted as guards for the Sixth Army's headquarters but also undertook more aggressive operations – two companies landed on Santiago Island at the northwest entrance to Lingayen Gulf to establish a radar station, while other detachments launched reconnaissance patrols into Luzon's mountainous and jungle-covered interior.

However, the most renowned Ranger operation of the campaign took place at the end of January after Mucci attended a meeting at Dagupan, the Sixth Army's headquarters, on the 27th and was ordered to free an estimated 500 US captives from a Japanese prison camp some 10 miles (16 km) east of Cabanatuan in the island's central plains. Many of the prisoners were survivors of the Japanese capture of the Philippines in 1942 and it was feared that they would either be moved or executed before they could be liberated by the forces committed to the ongoing ground offensive. Mucci felt that the infiltration of the whole battalion some 30 miles (48 km) behind enemy lines would be far too risky so selected his Company C under Captain Robert Prince and the 2nd Platoon of F Company for the raid – just 121 men. Filipino guerrillas were available to guide the Rangers to their target, while members of the Alamo Scouts, a specialist reconnaissance formation created by Krueger and named after the famed mission in his home town, San Antonio, Texas, kept the compound under observation.

The raid opened at 0500 hours on the 28th, when trucks transported the Rangers from their base at Calasio by way of Dagupan to Guimba, where they disembarked from their transporters. They next marched a few miles eastwards to Lobong, where they were met by 80 local guerrillas under Captain Eduardo Jonson. As darkness fell the raiders set off for their objective, negotiating the jungle paths leading eastwards three miles (5 km) south of Baloc. After crossing the Cabanatuan–San José road they plunged farther eastwards, crossing the Talavera River around midnight and then reached the Cabanatuan–Rizal road at 0400 hours on the 29th. Two hours later Mucci and his men halted at Balincarin, five miles (8 km) north of the camp, where they ate and rested – they had covered 25 miles in 24 hours. Mucci was joined by Captain Juan Pajota, who added 90 armed guerrillas and 160 porters to the raid. Pajota was also able to provide the carts that would be needed to move the sick and weakened prisoners back to friendly lines. At 1600 hours Mucci led his men due south towards Plateros, where he met two Alamo Scouts. They informed him that Cabanatuan was guarded by 500 Japanese troops

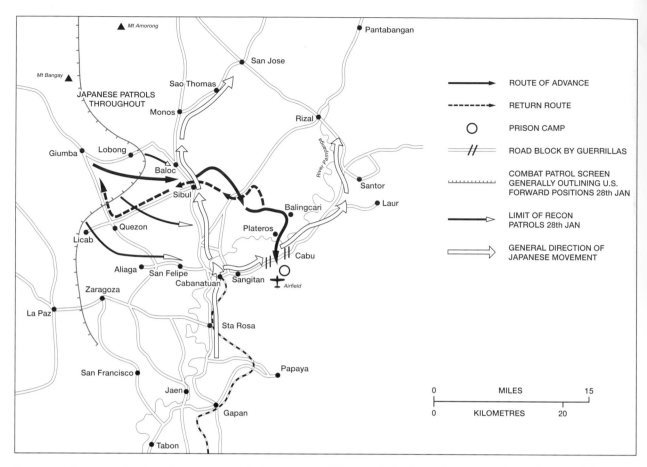

Above: The mission to rescue the prisoners from Cabanatuan.

and that an enemy division was falling back along a second road between Cabanatuan town and Rizal that ran close to the compound near Cabu. Mucci gained permission from Sixth Army headquarters to delay his attack until the next day to allow the enemy division to depart.

The raid devised by Mucci was complex, involving several distinct forces. Jonson's guerrillas and a six-man Ranger bazooka team established a blocking position at a point on the road some 800 yards (700 m) southwest of the camp to stop any Japanese advancing from Cabanatuan town. Similarly, Pajota's guerrillas set up positions on the same road but at Cabu bridge a mile (1.6 km) northeast of the compound to prevent the arrival of any of the 800-strong enemy garrison based at the latter town. Other guerrillas were detached to sever the camp's telephone lines to isolate it from outside help. Company F's 2nd Platoon under Lieutenant John Murphy infiltrated into positions close to the compound's eastern perimeter; its job was to neutralize two emplacements and a pair of observation towers at the moment when Company C began its attack through the main gate on the northern perimeter, which was also close to the huts holding the US prisoners. Speed was essential as any delay might have allowed the Japanese to execute their captives.

After leaving Platero during the afternoon of the 30th, the Rangers and guerrillas crossed the Pampanga River. The guerrillas then took up their blocking positions and the Rangers pushed on to the camp without being detected. The attack opened at around 1945 and was heralded by the cutting of the telephone lines and Murphy's diversionary assault on the eastern perimeter. Company C, in positions just 20 yards from the main gate, then attacked, rapidly killing sentries and men resting in nearby barracks. The

company's various assault sections now split up to carry out various tasks and fanned out through the complex: four tanks and two trucks were destroyed; radios were smashed; the prisoners released and helped out of the compound. The raid was completed in a mere 30 minutes; Prince fired a single red flare to start the withdrawal. Ranger casualties had been remarkably light with just a few men wounded but a medical officer, Captain James Fisher, was mortally wounded by a mortar fragment and a second man, Roy Sweezy, fell victim to friendly rifle fire. A mile outside the now-burning camp, the captain fired a second flare, which was the signal for the two blocking parties to abandon their positions. Jonson had no difficulties and fell in behind the withdrawing Rangers and liberated prisoners, but Pejota took around an hour to extricate his men from a bitter firefight with an unexpectedly large Japanese force of 2,000 men from Cebu.

The withdrawing column first renegotiated the Pampanga River, where carts were waiting for the sick and wounded, and then reached Plateros, where Fisher succumbed to his wounds the next day in the temporary field hospital he himself had previously established. The column began the next stage of journey back to friendly lines at 2130, and, as more and more carts were made available, passed through Balincarin. Flank and rear guards were deployed to slow the pursuit of the Japanese and, although the column moved slowly on a course that paralleled but was south of that used to reach the prison camp, Mucci was fortunate in that he would not have as far to go as expected because, on the morning of the 31st, he learned that the front line had been pushed beyond Guimba and Lobong since he had left for the operation. The Rangers' first contact with Sixth Army units occurred at Talavera town, where ambulances and other transports were gathered to move the sick and wounded to nearby hospitals at Guimba. Some 513 prisoners had been brought out of captivity while two Rangers had been killed and 10 wounded. The Cabanatuan raid was a classic Ranger operation and earned the gratitude of MacArthur who remarked that: 'no incident of this war has given me greater satisfaction than the Ranger rescue of these Americans.' Aside from the acclaim of the popular press back home, those involved received other awards. C Company and F Company's 2nd Platoon earned Presidential Unit Citations. Mucci and Prince received the Distinguished Service Cross, every

Above: Escorting PoWs released from Cabanatuan prison on Luzon, Philippines, January 1945.

Below: January 30, 1945. Donald A. Adams of 6th Rangers and Abe Abraham, ex-PoW.

MERRILL'S MARAUDERS

An American Ranger-style force, the 5307th Composite Provisional Unit was formed in India in 1943 and trained under the direction of Orde Wingate, the Chindit leader. Nicknamed 'Merrill's Marauders', after their leader, Brigadier-General Frank Merrill, they campaigned brilliantly, earning a Presidential Unit Citation. Outnumbered, without heavy weapons, they defeated the veterans of the Japanese 18th Division who had conquered Singapore and Malaya in 1941. They disrupted enemy supply and communication lines, and finally captured Myitkina Airfield, the only all-weather airfield in Burma. While in Burma they trained Gurkhas and Kachins, such as those illustrated here.

Below right: US-trained Gurkha Ranger on guard at Myitkina, January 18, 1945.

Below: Gurkha and Kachin training session underway at Myitkina.

other officer the Silver Star, and every enlisted man the Bronze Star.

The Cabanatuan mission was also the high point of the 6th Battalion's participation in the Pacific campaign, but the unit continued to operate in the Philippines until the end of the war. A variety of operations were conducted, chiefly hit-and-run raids, reconnaissance, and clearing Luzon's highland interior. Such operations were conducted by individual companies. In April, for example, one was used to block a Japanese withdrawal from the eastern sector of Luzon, while beginning in May another was sent on a long-range mission into the north of the island. This involved the battalion's Company B infiltrating some 200 miles (320 km) behind enemy lines to reach Appari on the island's north coast and then aid an assault landing by the US 11th Airborne Division. After the landings the Rangers operated with the paratroopers as they pushed southwards from Appari down the valley of the Cagayan River to link up with the US 37th Infantry Division in what was one of the last major attacks of the campaign.

Following the Japanese surrender in August 1945 the battalion was earmarked for occupation duties, although 139 men had already been demobilized on August 20. The remainder left Luzon for Japan on September 15 and landed at Honshu's Wakayama Beach 10 days later. The battalion established a base that was christened Camp Fisher, after the doctor killed in the withdrawal from Cabanatuan, but its occupation duties were neither onerous nor prolonged. At the end of November the battalion paraded for a final time before Krueger and it was formally deactivated on December 20, thereby ending the story of the Rangers in World War II.

AWARDS

Unit	Award	Location	Date
1st Rangers (**1**)	Presidential Unit Citation	El Guettar	1943
	Presidential Unit Citation	Salerno	1943
2nd Rangers (**2**)	Presidential Unit Citation	Pointe du Hoc	1944
	Croix de Guerre	Pointe du Hoc	1944
3rd Rangers (**3**)	Presidential Unit Citation	Salerno	1943
4th Rangers (**4**)			
5th Rangers (**5**)	Presidential Unit Citation	Pointe du Hoc	1944
	Croix de Guerre	Pointe du Hoc	1944
	Presidential Unit Citation	Irsch–Zerf	1945
6th Rangers (**6**)	Presidential Unit Citation	Cabanatuan (**7**)	1945
	Presidential Unit Citation	Philippines	1944–45

Notes

1 Participated in six campaigns, including four amphibious assaults.
2 Participated in five campaigns, including one amphibious assault.
3 Participated in four campaigns, including three amphibious assaults.
4 Participated in four campaigns, including three amphibious assaults.
5 Participated in five campaigns, including one amphibious assault.
6 Participated in three campaigns, including one amphibious assault.
7 Awarded to Company C and 2nd Platoon, Company F.

DARBY'S FAREWELL

The 1st, 3rd and 4th Rangers were officially deactivated in late 1944 following their return to the United States and in April 1945 Darby penned a heart-felt letter (in the event shortly before his own death) to those who had survived the battles in Europe:

'… As your commanding officer, I am justly proud to have led such an outstanding group of American fighting men. Never was I more sad than on the day of our parting. Never was I more content than being with you on our many exciting operations. You trained hard, you fought hard, and always you gave your best regardless of discomfort or danger. From the great Allied raid at Dieppe through the exacting, bitter campaigns culminating with the Anzio beachhead battles, the 1st, 3rd, and 4th Ranger Battalions have performed in a capacity unsurpassed by the highest traditions of the American Army. Your record speaks for itself.

We – the living Rangers – will never forget our fallen comrades. They and the ideals for which they fought will remain ever present among us, for we fully understand the extent of their heroic sacrifices. We will carry their spirit with us into all walks of life, into all corners of America. Our hearts join together in sorrow for their loss; but also our hearts swell with pride to have fought alongside such valiant men. They will never be considered dead, for they live with us in spirit …

No better way can I sum up my feelings of pride for your splendid achievements than to state this: Commanding the Rangers was like driving a team of very high-spirited horses. No effort was needed to get them to go forward. The problem was to hold them in check. Good luck, Rangers, and may your futures be crowned with deserving success.'

INSIGNIA, CLOTHING & EQUIPMENT

Above right: Rangers' shoulder flashes. The first (left)was designed by Sgt. Anthony Fleet in 1942. Each of the six battalions wore an unofficial scroll like this one – made official in 1987. The lozenge shape (middle) was only worn by members of 2nd and 5th Rangers. The third (right) was used by 29th Rangers. Underneath is the unofficial flash of 'Merrill's Marauders'.

Right: Re-enactment view of Operation Torch uniforms – M1942 herringbone twill suits, M1 helmets, M1928 haversacks, and gasmasks carried slung across their chests. The man on the right carries an M1 .30 cal rifle; the one on the left an M1928A1 Thompson submachine gun. Note US identification armbands.

Below: Corporal 'Zip' Koons displays his 1st Ranger Battalion shoulder flash.

The Rangers who saw service in World War II generally wore uniforms and carried weapons that were standard throughout the US Army. However, as the text below reveals there were exceptions to this that grew out of their specialist role and, with regard to uniform, because of their initial attachment to British units. Members of the various battalions also wore standard rank insignia and the like but did adopt a range of unit cloth badges that marked them out as Rangers.

INSIGNIA

The insignia most used to identify members of the six main Ranger Battalions during World War II was the scroll worn singly on the wearer's upper left shoulder. This was originally an unofficial design created for the 1st Battalion in late 1942 by Sergeant Anthony Fleet but it was later copied by the other battalions and gained acceptance with the US military authorities. Fleet's badge comprised a very dark blue/black scroll-shaped background with white lettering enclosed in a edging in the form of a thin red line. The title 'Ranger' appeared in the centre with the unit's number to the viewer's left and the abbreviation 'BN' for battalion on the right. The cloth patches were generally manufactured locally and were not always readily available so it is not uncommon to see photos of Rangers without the device.

During Operation Torch in North Africa in November 1942, the 1st Battalion wore special badges to indicate their nationality to the opposing Vichy French, as it was thought that they were less likely to fire on US troops. A detachable US flag was worn on the left shoulder and a plain white band was worn about midway between the elbow and shoulder of one, or sometimes both, arms.

In contrast to the more common scroll device, the short-lived 29th Provisional Ranger Battalion wore an entirely different scroll comprising a small red shoulder tab with the words '29th Ranger' in mid-blue lettering. This was sometimes worn above the emblem of the US 29th Infantry Division, a green-edged circle divided into blue and grey halves by an S-shaped curve, from the ranks of which the battalion's recruits were drawn.

A second cloth shoulder insignia was officially approved for all of the Ranger battalions in July 1943, although it appears only to have been worn by the 2nd and 5th Battalions, and began to appear the following September. It consisted of a lozenge-shaped piece of light blue cloth with gold-yellow edging and the title 'Rangers' in the centre rendered in the same colour. An unofficial version of the design with two gold-yellow edges was worn by members of the 5th Battalion from September 1943 but was replaced by the prescribed version after a couple of months. Both symbols were nicknamed the Blue Sunoco as they bore a close similarity to the corporate logo of the

Above: Wet weather gear in Scotland, October 31, 1942. Note the 'new' M1 helmet rather than the British-style M1917A1. The original rubberised cotton ponchos soon gave way to resin-coated nylon fabric. They didn't have hoods – just a drawstring – or sleeves – snap fasteners allowed them to be gathered around the arms. All had metal grommets to allow them to be used as tent shelters.

US Sunoco Oil Company and, unlike the scroll, sometimes appeared on both shoulders. The 2nd and 5th Battalions abandoned their Blue Sunoco designs during the summer of 1945, only after the war in Europe had ended, when they adopted the standard scroll.

During the assault on the Pointe du Hoc the Rangers of both battalions had field identification symbols painted onto the back of their helmets. These consisted of a gold-yellow lozenge with the battalion number in black in the centre. Officers were further identified by a short, broad vertical white band running behind the lozenge, while non-commissioned officers had a similar device but running horizontally.

CLOTHING

For the most part the Rangers wore standard US military dress throughout the war. When training in Scotland, they were mostly seen in the one-piece herring-bone work suit in olive drab. The British-style M1917A1 helmet was used during this period but was replaced by the ubiquitous M1 during the latter part of 1942. For operations in North Africa, Rangers wore serge olive drab trousers, wool shirts of a similar colour, the M1 helmet and web gaiters and in warm weather they generally fought in this shirt-sleeve order. However, as desert nights can be cold, they were often seen dressed in the M1941 jacket, a waist-length single-breasted design, that proved only moderately successful in combating the night-time temperatures. It was not uncommon for Rangers to wear extra items of clothing – pullovers, scarves and the olive knit cap or beanie – for additional warmth. The jacket issued to members of armoured units, a waist-length design with knitted collar and cuff, was also highly prized as it had a warmer lining and offered greater protection from the weather. However, for the most part, the Rangers soldiered on with the M1941 through Sicily, Italy and D-Day, but many adopted the M1943 woollen field jacket when it became available as this design offered better protection against the winter weather encountered during the final stages of the campaign in Europe.

For its operations in the Pacific the 6th Rangers mostly wore the lightweight M1943 herring-bone fatigues and for the Cabanatuan raid its headgear comprised the M1941 field cap.

Probably almost uniquely, some Rangers also wore British battledress for a time. The party of men who fought at Dieppe in 1942 had much the same uniform as the Commando units to which they were attached and the same was true of members of the 29th Ranger Battalion when they participated in raids against Occupied Europe.

WEAPONS

The Rangers were essentially fast-moving light infantry and generally lacked support weapons that were more powerful than light/medium machine guns, mortars and bazookas. Their small arms were generally standard issue and comparable to those carried by other US infantry units. If their firepower needed to be boosted, they were supported by units or detachments that could provide the necessary weapons.

Pistols, Rifles and Sub-machine Guns

When the 1st Battalion arrived in Scotland for training, the men were equipped with the M1903A1 bolt-action Springfield rifle but this was quickly replaced by the .30-calibre Garand M1 semi-automatic from the autumn of 1942 and this became the mainstay of the individual Ranger's firepower for the remainder of the war, although some hung on to the Springfield for a time. Among these men were snipers, one of whom was attached to the headquarters of each platoon, who continued to use a modified version of the M1903 Springfield, the A, fitted with a telescope sight such as the M73B. When it became available, the Rangers also adopted the shorter M1 carbine. The most popular sub-machine gun was the excellent .45 calibre M1 Thompson, which was originally held at battalion level and issued to individual Rangers when necessary. The Rangers used the 50-round drum magazine in their early days but it proved cumbersome and was replaced by the 20- or 30-round box magazine. The most popular pistol was M1911A1 automatic.

Machine Guns

The first Ranger battalions were issued with 23 .30-calibre tripod-mounted Browning M1919A4 light machine guns. These were wholly satisfactory weapons, capable of firing around 500 rounds per minute from 250-round belts, but not entirely suited to Ranger-style operations as they were comparatively heavy and not easy to move around the battlefield at speed. More practical for giving direct close support during an attack was the M1918A2 Browning Automatic Rifle (BAR). This was operated by a single Ranger

Above: T/Sgt. John S. Rembecki does some paperwork in camp in England, October 1942. Note the early war equipment – British-style M1917A1 helmet.

Right: This close-up shows a detail of the front of the M1926 US Navy lifebelt, worn under an assault vest.

Below: Rear view of the two soldiers seen on page 67. Note the five-magazine pouch for the Thompson and the waterbottle of the man on the right, and the M1923 cartridge belt of man at the left..

Far right: A re-enactment of the Pointe du Hoc mission. Note the extremely light combat gear carried – he has little more than a water bottle and a Thompson. Note the Airborne jump boots that were often used by Rangers.

Above: January 20, 1943 – a Ranger exercise in North
Africa.

Right: Going over the rail of the transport to the assault
craft, November 8, 1942.

Opposite: Speed march training, 1st Rangers North Africa,
December 5, 1942. At right, Corporal Chester Fisches of
Clinton, Idaho, carries his rifle over his shoulder. He is
bareheaded in the heat, and wears the shirt sleeve order so
often seen in North Africa, wool shirt, trousers, boots, M1938
webbing gaiters. He has an M1923 rifleman's, s web cartridge
belt and an M1 rifle. At left, is similarly clad Private Edward
T. Calhoun of Campbelleville, Kentucky.

SCALING THE POINTE DU HOC

The three companies of the 2nd Ranger Battalion under Lieutenant Colonel James Rudder tasked with scaling the 100-foot (30 m) cliffs of the Pointe du Hoc faced one of the most difficult tasks of D-Day. Aware that speed was essential to their success, they were issued with various ingenious devices that were designed to lessen the difficulties of reaching the summit of their target as quickly as possible.

The Rangers came ashore in several LCAs (Landing Craft, Assault) that had each been fitted with three pairs of rockets. One pair was capable of throwing a ¾-inch (7 mm) diameter rope attached to a grapnel to heights of around 200 feet (70 m); the second deployed similar rope lines but these were fitted with 2-inch wooden toggles every foot or so; and the third pair launched light rope ladders that had rungs every two feet. However, many of the ropes became thoroughly sodden during the final approach to the beach and proved far too heavy to be lifted to the cliff-top when fired. When these devices failed, the Rangers resorted to smaller hand-held versions with a range of around 100 feet (30 m) and some of these did reach the summit. The LCAs also carried self-assembly ladders ashore. These consisted of 4-foot (1.2 m) tubular sections that could be fitted together to complete a 112-foot (34 m) ladder. For the Pointe du Hoc assault the Rangers pre-assembled 16-foot (5 m) sections to hasten the process of completing the ladders once they were at the base of the cliffs.

The most extraordinary items of equipment available to the Rangers were specially customized DUKW amphibians. Although these were normally deployed to carry troops or supplies, on D-Day the Rangers were accompanied by two DUKWs fitted with turntable-mounted extendable ladders capable of reaching heights of around 100 feet (30 m) that had been acquired from the London Fire Brigade. The top of each ladder was fitted with a pair of Lewis guns designed to give the climbers a measure of fire support. Although the converted DUKWs had performed to expectation on exercises before June 6, on the actual day they failed at the first hurdle. They were unable to reach the foot of the cliffs due to their inability to cross the narrow shell-blasted beach that was littered with large sections of the cliff that had been detached by the pre-landing naval bombardment.

Since much of the specialist climbing equipment was unsatisfactory for the intended task, the Rangers resorted to other methods. Some were able to use ordinary climbing ropes or put together sections of toggle ropes, several of which were cut by the Germans as the Rangers scaled the heights, while others resorted to gouging out hand and foot holds in the face using their hands and combat knives. In the event many Rangers were killed or wounded in the climb and a good number needed several attempts to reach the summit.

Right: Three more re-enactment views of Rudder's 2nd Rangers assaulting Pointe du Hoc. Note in particular the '2' in an orange diamond on the back of the helmet identifying the unit. This was seen with the 2nd and 5th Rangers. While the ladder looks efficient, in fact the Rangers found the specialist climbing equipment did not work as planned (as described in the box above). Note also the rear of the US Navy lifebelt on man at left, and the US assault vest worn by the two lower men (in two different colours).

Right: Radio report being prepared by a 5th Rangers' team 'somewhere in France', August 17, 1944.

Below right: Ranger mortar section, December 2, 1942, North Africa.

Overleaf: Another re-enactment view of 2nd Rangers at Pointe du Hoc.

who might carry up to 12 20-round magazines on the specially designed M1937 belt. Although the BAR was fitted with a bipod, it was not uncommon for Rangers to remove the stabilizing device to reduce the weapon's weight and make it easier to wield.

Mortars

The Rangers relied on two main types of mortar. Typically, a battalion was issued with six of the larger calibre 81 mm M1 types and three times as many of the smaller 60 mm M2 version of the weapon.

Anti-tank Weapons

For tank-killing the earliest Ranger battalions relied on the generally unsatisfactory British-designed .55-calibre Boys anti-tank rifle fitted with a five-round magazine. The official establishment called for a battalion to have 20 of these weapons but their obsolescence was evident in the early stages of the war and the Rangers came to rely on the 2.36-inch M1 rocket-launcher, the famed bazooka, which packed a much better punch, not only for attacking tanks but also for neutralizing fixed defences.

Grenades and Demolitions

As with other equipment, the Rangers were issued with standard anti-personnel grenades. Among these were the M6 fragmentation grenade and the more unusual M6 CN-DM devices filled with tear or vomiting gas. Rifle grenades were also available. For example the M1919 Springfield could be fitted with the M1 launcher to fire the M9 anti-tank grenade. Rangers were trained in the use of bangalore torpedoes, which were primarily used for clearing paths through minefields or cutting barbed wire entanglements. They consisted of 1½-inch or 2-inch diameter 8-foot tubes filled with 10 or 12 lb of explosives. Depending on the width of the obstruction, several sections could be fitted together in much the same way as a socket bayonet is fixed to a rifle and an igniter fitted to the end nearest the user. A nose plug was fitted to the front portion to allow the whole device to be pushed more easily through any obstruction. The Rangers also employed the pole charge on occasion. This close-quarters device was used for pushing through the observation slits and fire ports of pill-boxes and consisted of a pair of Mk IIIA1 percussion grenades fixed to a length of tent pole.

Below: A Korean War photograph, but it shows off the Browning Automatic Rifle which was the main support weapon for Ranger units in World War II. Here it is used with its bipod; this was often discarded in action because of its weight. BAR gunners wore the M1937 automatic rifleman's belt which had six web pockets, each holding two 20-round magazines.

PEOPLE

WILLIAM O. DARBY (1911–45)

Darby had a conventional upbringing in Fort Smith, Arkansas, and secured a place at West Point in part thanks to the intervention of a local member of Congress, Otis Wingo. A member of the class of 1933, he had an exemplary record as a student and on his graduation was commissioned as a second lieutenant in the 1st Battalion, 82nd Field Artillery Regiment, which was part of the 1st Cavalry Division and based at Fort Bliss, Texas. Over the following years Darby attended various training courses and gained sufficient leadership skills to be promoted to captain on October 1, 1940. In 1941 he gained his first experiences of amphibious assault techniques when he attended exercises in Puerto Rico and at the New River training facility in North Carolina. During November Darby was ordered to Hawaii but had not arrived by the time of the Japanese surprise attack on December 7 and, following the US declaration of war, he was ordered to report to Major General Russell Hartle's 34th Infantry Division, which sailed for Northern Ireland on January 15, 1942.

Hartle was made commander of the US Army Northern Ireland on the 27th with Darby as his aide, but the young officer was looking for a more active role and on

Left: Fort Jackson, April 24, 1943, sees more PE. The men are wearing the distinctive field hat so popular with Merrill's Marauders.

Below left: October 8, 1944. 6th Rangers march to its embarkation point in New Guinea preparatory to assault Dinagat Island. This photograph gives a good idea of the tropical clothing – herringbone fatigues and camouflaged helmet covers.

Below: Lt-Col. W. O. Darby in the field, North Africa, December 12, 1942.

WORLD WAR II RANGER COMMANDERS

1st Battalion
Major William O. Darby (**1**)
Major John Dobson (**2**)

2nd Battalion
Lieutenant Colonel William C. Saffarans
Major L. E. McDonald
Lieutenant Colonel James E. Rudder
Major George S. Williams

3rd Battalion
Major Herman Dammer
Major Alvah Miller (**3**)

4th Battalion
Major Roy Murray

5th Battalion
Major Owen H. Carter
Lieutenant Colonel Max Schneider
Lieutenant-Colonel Richard Sullivan

6th Battalion
Lieutenant Colonel Henry A. Mucci
Major Robert Garrett

29th Provisional Ranger Battalion
Major Randolph Millholland

(**1**) died of wounds, posthumously promoted brigadier-general
(**2**) badly wounded at Anzio
(**3**) killed at Anzio

Below: Darby epitomised the Rangers of the early war years and it was his drive that ensured they were prepared to a high standard and performed as expected. An exceptional leader, Derby was decorated a number of times – here he wears the the ribbon the British Distinguished Service Order presented to him for heroism above and beyond the call of duty. He is seen after Anzio, when his command was wiped out, as CO of 179th Infantry Regiment, part of 45th Infantry Division, before he took on a staff role.

June 8 he was appointed to lead a new unit, which was to become the 1st Ranger Battalion. Between the summer of 1942 and early 1944 Darby was the dominant figure in the Rangers. He took part in several major operations – Operation Torch, the Tunisian campaign, Sicily, Salerno, and Anzio, and oversaw the expansion of his command from one to three battalions. Darby received numerous awards, including a Silver Star for the Sened night attack, a Distinguished Service Medal for the action at El Guettar, and a Distinguished Service Cross for the landings at Gela in Sicily. In the autumn of 1944 he received several other awards, among them the Legion of Merit, the Croix de Guerre, the Soviet Union's Order of Kutuzov, Third Class, and the Oak Leaf Cluster to the Purple Heart. However, Anzio marked his last action with the Rangers. Following the virtual destruction of all three battalions in late January 1944, he was left without a command and on February 16 was assigned to the US 45th Infantry Division's severely understrength 179th Infantry Regiment, leading it for the next two months. Thanks to the intervention of General Mark Clark, Darby was assigned to the Operations Division of the War Department General Staff and left Anzio for Washington during April. Over the following several months he undertook staff duties that were not particularly to his liking but his requests for a return to a more active role were initially turned down.

Darby nevertheless continued to request a transfer and finally gained permission to return overseas on March 29, 1945. He had a roving commission to study the effectiveness of air support during ground operations and decided to return to Italy to join the 10th Mountain Division under Major General George P. Hayes, formerly Darby's commander when he had served with the 99th Field Artillery Regiment during 1940–41. Shortly after Darby's arrival the division's assistant commander was wounded and Darby, with Hayes' support, was able to take his place. In late April, the division was attacking up the east side of Lake Garda in the north of Italy and on the late afternoon of the 30th after the defeat of a German counterattack, Darby decided to go forward to inspect one of the numerous tunnels through which ran the lakeside road and where the enemy advance had been blocked. All seemed quiet as he left a command post at a hotel in Torbole, but as Darby was preparing to board a waiting jeep a shell landed within 10 yards. Darby's heart was hit by a small fragment and he died of his wounds within a few minutes without regaining consciousness. On the same day he died, Darby's name appeared in a list of officers who had been recommended for promotion. Secretary of War Stimson broke with existing practice and Darby's name remained on the list. He was posthumously promoted to the rank of brigadier general. Darby's undoubted leadership skills were perhaps best summed up by General Lucian Truscott, who was moved to write shortly after his death that he had 'Never in this war... known a more gallant, heroic officer.'

HENRY MUCCI (1911–97)

Henry Andrew Mucci, a graduate of the West Point Class of 1936, had been present at the attack on Pearl Harbor in December 1941, when he was the provost marshal in Honolulu. When in 1944 he took charge of the newly formed 6th Ranger Battalion at the age of 33, he quickly gained two nicknames: 'Little MacArthur', because he smoked a pipe similar to that used by the commanding general in the theatre, and 'Ham', an affectionate play on his initials that reflected his sometimes theatrical style of leadership. However, Mucci was a strict disciplinarian, supremely fit, and ambitious for his new battalion. He led it with distinction during the Philippines campaign, most notably during the rescue mission at Cabanatuan in early 1945. After the war, Mucci returned to his hometown, Bridgeport, Connecticut, and received a rapturous hero's welcome from 50,000 local citizens for his leadership of the Cabanatuan operation. Following a failed attempt to be elected to Congress, he later became a representative for an oil company from Canada and worked in the Far East, although there were rumours, which he strenuously denied, that he was actually an undercover operative for the Central Intelligence Agency. He died aged 86 after suffering complications from a hip fracture that occurred while swimming in rough seas near his final home in Melbourne, Florida.

Above: A conference aboard the *Winchester Castle*, January 1944. From left to right: ship's captain S. F. Newdigate; Lt-Col. William P. Yarborough, CO of 509th Parachute Infantry Battalion; and Lt-Col. Roy A. Murray, CO of 4th Ranger Battalion.

JAMES E. RUDDER (1910–70)

Texas-born Rudder attended the John Tarleton Agricultural College in 1928 and 1929 but then studied at Texas A&M University, graduating with a degree in industrial education. He was subsequently commissioned second lieutenant in the US Army Reserve, while working as a teacher and football coach at Tarleton. He was called up in 1941 and two years later, as a lieutenant colonel, was assigned to command the 2nd Ranger Battalion. On D-Day he led the crucial and difficult assault on the Pointe du Hoc, a successful operation but one that saw Rudder wounded twice. He led the battalion over the following six months during operations to liberate northwest Europe and was then transferred to command the 109th Infantry Regiment, which saw action during that winter's Battle of the Bulge. By the war's end Rudder was a full colonel and had been

awarded numerous medals, including the Distinguished Service Cross, Legion of Merit, Silver Star, and the French Legion of Honour with Croix de Guerre and Palm. Rudder was the mayor of Brady, Texas, between 1946 and 1952, and for a year was vice-president of the Brady Aviation Company. In early 1955, he became a commissioner overseeing the Veterans' Land Program and held the post for the next three years, before becoming vice-president of Texas A&M. In 1959 he became the university's president and in 1965 became president of the entire A&M system, a position he held until his death. In his later years Rudder was successively promoted to brigadier general and major general in the US Army Reserve and in 1967 his distinguished career was crowned by President Lyndon Johnson awarding him the Distinguished Service Medal.

LUCIAN K. TRUSCOTT JR. (1895–1965)

Texas-born Truscott was a leading figure in the creation of the Rangers and had a distinguished career as a senior field commander during World War II. He joined the US Army in 1917 and spent his early years as a cavalry officer before being attached to the 13th Armored Regiment in 1940. In May 1942 he was promoted to the rank of brigadier general and assigned to the Allied Combined Operations staff under Britain's Lord Louis Mountbatten. During this period he analysed the Commandos and recommended that the United States raise a similar force, a decision that led directly to the creation of the Rangers. Truscott oversaw their first operation – the raid in force on Dieppe in August – but was then transferred to other assignments. As commander of the 3rd Infantry Division, which fought alongside the Rangers on occasion, he took part in the invasions of Sicily, Salerno and Anzio in 1943. In February 1944 he took command of the VI Corps at Anzio and subsequently led it during the invasion of southern France. In December 1944 he returned to Italy to take charge of the Fifth Army during the final stages of the campaign. After a spell as commander of the US Third Army in Bavaria he returned to the United States in 1946 and retired the following year.

Above: Brigadier General Truscott on July 2, 1943, when in command of US 3rd Infantry Division.

Right: 1st Sgt Warren E. Evans – the official caption notes him as 6ft 4in in height, 24 years old, native of Aberdeen, South Dakota, ex-football player – being congratulated by Brigadier-General L. K. Truscott, August 1942.

POSTWAR

KOREA – RANGER HOPES DASHED

The swift disbandment of the six Ranger battalions at the end of World War II reflected the general scaling down of US armed forces and a growing emphasis on nuclear deterrence in the era of the Cold War at the expense of conventional forces. However, the value of specialist ground troops became apparent with the outbreak of the Korean War in June 1950. The US Army's Chief of Staff, General J. Lawton Collins, visited South Korea and on his return to the United States recommended the formation of so-called Marauder Companies. A formal request was issued on August 29, on the basis that each company should comprise five officers and 107 men skilled in reconnaissance and behind-the-lines missions and be attached to individual divisions. Following a suggestion that the new units would be better named Airborne Ranger Companies, volunteers from the 11th and 82nd Airborne Divisions assembled at Fort Benning, Georgia, where Colonel John Van Houten had been placed in charge of the newly activated Ranger Training Center (Airborne). The first four companies completed their six-week training course on November 11. In total 15 Airborne Ranger Companies were activated from late October 1950 to late February 1951 but only six served in Korea; the remainder stayed in the United States or were stationed elsewhere overseas, chiefly West Germany and Japan.

The companies that fought in Korea from December 1950 undertook a range of missions, such as intelligence-gathering, raids and ambushes to collect prisoners, and as spearhead infantry. Mostly these were small-scale and hazardous affairs – one recruit remarked that, 'for the Rangers in Korea, fighting outnumbered and surrounded was routine' – but the Rangers were occasionally involved in larger operations. The largest occurred on March 23, 1951, when the 2nd and 4th Airborne Ranger Companies parachuted alongside the 187th Airborne Regimental Combat Team in the vicinity of Munsan-ni to block the retreat of North Korean and Chinese troops from Seoul, the South Korean capital,

Below: March 6, 1951– a Ranger patrol briefing.

which had just been liberated by UN forces for the second time. The action, the only such airborne mission of the war, was not wholly successful and many of the enemy forces escaped the attempted encirclement.

By mid-1951 the seesaw war of movement in Korea had ended and both sides established fixed positions along what the UN forces christened the Main Line of Resistance. It was not a happy time for the Rangers; there were undoubted problems with logistical support as they relied on the divisions they served with for supplies, and doubts were expressed on the worth of such units in a static war. In July 1951 orders were issued to deactivate the various companies. Those in Korea were disbanded on August 1, while those serving elsewhere followed between September and December. The Ranger Training Command was inactivated on October 17 but hopes that the Rangers might rise again came with the creation of the Ranger Department the same month. Its role was to train officers and non-commissioned officers who could pass on Ranger skills to others when they were returned to their parent formation.

Above: M16 rifle at the ready, a camouflaged 75th Ranger walks point on an operation in Tuyen Duc province, March 4, 1970.

THE COLD WAR AND VIETNAM

From the late 1950s the leading members of NATO began programmes to develop special forces capable of operations deep behind enemy – Warsaw Pact – lines. Capable of acting wholly independently, they were composed of very small units that were known as Long Range Reconnaissance Patrols (LRRPs) or, in the case of the United States, Long Range Patrols (LRPs), and their chief function was reconnaissance and intelligence-gathering. The first LRPs were raised to test the concept, appearing in around 1958, and two companies were formally activated in West Germany on July 15, 1961. They had a checkered career, being deactivated four years later, re-attached to a new unit, and then transferred back to the United States in 1968.

Renewed impetus to develop the LRP idea came with the commitment of US ground forces to Vietnam, where the need for specialist units to conduct a whole range of behind-the-lines operations became apparent. Individual divisions and corps began to activate LRP-style patrols and platoons. Official recognition of their value came in late 1967, when the US military authorities formally ordered the creation of LRPs. These were either of company strength, 118 men, when attached to a division or larger formation, or of reinforced platoon strength, around 61 men, if serving with a brigade. The new LRPs did not have a parent regiment or links with any previous force and so they were assigned to the 75th Infantry Regiment, which had a lineage associated with Merrill's Marauders, on February 1, 1969, and all LRPs were redesignated as 'Ranger'. The LRPs could not be given the honours or lineage of the Rangers of World War II as the traditions had been passed to the US Special Forces (Green Berets) in April 1960. The Ranger companies in Vietnam suffered the same fate as their predecessors – they were inactivated between 1969 and 1972.

PEACEKEEPING AND THE MIDDLE EAST

The completion of the withdrawal of US ground forces from Vietnam in 1973 was preceded by a reduction in Ranger strength, with just two companies, A and B, remaining in the United States. However, interest in the concept was renewed by the outbreak of the Yom Kippur War between Israel and Egypt, which threatened to destabilize the Middle East and involve the superpowers in direct confrontation. The US military acknowledged that it lacked lightly equipped forces mobile enough to be quickly sent to any trouble spot and the following year, General Creighton Abrams, the US Army's Chief of Staff, ordered the formation of the 1st and 2nd Battalions, 75th Infantry (Rangers) based around men from the surviving Ranger companies. the 1st Battalion was activated at Fort Benning, Georgia, on January 31, 1974, and the 2nd Battalion followed at Fort Lewis, Washington, on October 1.

The revitalized Rangers undertook their first combat assignment on April 28–29, 1980, during Operation Eagle Claw, the abortive attempt to rescue US hostages held in Teheran by the fundamentalist Islamic regime of Iran. The complex night-time operation involved a wide range of US special forces but only Company C of the Rangers' 1st Battalion was involved in the mission. Its role was to seize a desert airfield at Manzariyeh, some 35 miles (55 km) southwest of the Iranian capital, from where the hostages would be flown to safety in C-141 Starlifters after being rescued from the US embassy compound in the capital. Eagle Claw ended disastrously, when two of the helicopters detailed to move the hostage rescuers to their target failed to reach a rendezvous point known as Desert One due to mechanical problems and then one of the six that reached the position suffered similar difficulties. The lack of functioning helicopters made it impossible to move the rescue teams to Teheran and a withdrawal was ordered. During its execution a collision destroyed a C-130 and a Sea Stallion, forcing the remaining US forces present to abandon the surviving helicopters and withdraw in C-130 transports.

The failure of Eagle Claw was an international embarrassment, but the Rangers' next mission in October 1983 was much more successful. A palace coup ousted the populist, moderately left-wing leader of the Caribbean island of Grenada, Prime Minister Maurice Bishop, and his subsequent execution led the US authorities to use the unrest as a pretext to occupy Grenada. There were worries about the fate of US students attending various campuses on the island but, more importantly, its ongoing and strengthening ties with Cuba were of serious geopolitical concern. President Ronald Reagan, with support from other Caribbean leaders, ordered the deployment of troops to overthrow the new revolutionary regime and rescue the students.

Some 500 Rangers drawn from both battalions took part in the operation, which was code-named Urgent Fury and opened on the 25th. The Rangers' role was to secure the airfield nearing completion at Point Salinas on the island's southeast tip so that 750 men of the 82nd Airborne Division could land. The Rangers' parachute assault at around 0530 hours was met by heavy ground fire from local defence forces and hastily armed Cuban construction workers, but the area was quickly secured for the loss of five Rangers killed and six wounded. The assault teams next moved on the nearby True Blue Campus close to the eastern end of the airfield and within two hours had rescued 138 US medical students. The same feat was accomplished the next day, when 224 students were freed from Grand Anse campus, a few miles south of St. George, Grenada's capital. The Rangers' final operation on Grenada took place on the 27th, when an airmobile assault was launched against Calivigny Barracks outside St. George. Despite losing three men killed and five wounded when three of their four Black Hawk helicopters collided on landing, the surviving Rangers secured the objective.

Grenada and the possibility of similar operations in the future gave further impetus to the development of the Rangers. On October 3, 1984, the existing two units were strengthened by the activation of the 3rd Battalion and a regimental headquarters at Fort Benning, Georgia, with the whole force being named the 75th Infantry Regiment (Ranger). Two years later, on April 17, the three battalions were renamed the 75th Ranger Regiment, receiving all of the honours and the lineage of Ranger units that had served in World War II and Korea but sharing them with the Special Forces.

Above: The Rangers became airborne after World War II. This photograph is of trainees dropping at Fort Benning in 1950.

Above: The training is as arduous as ever. Here SFC William S. Brown demonstrates the use of the M60 machine gune while executing the Australian rappel at Fort Benning.

The Rangers' next major mission was Operation Just Cause on December 20, 1989, a multi-pronged US operation to overthrow the Panamanian dictator General Manuel Noriega, bring him to trial on charges of involvement in the illegal drugs trade, and maintain the free flow of shipping though the Panama Canal. They provided the bulk of Task Force Red, which was to seize various positions around Panama City at the Pacific entrance to the canal as a spearhead for the follow-on Task Force Pacific.

The 1st Battalion, along with the 3rd Battalion's Company C and headquarters detachment Team Gold, was code-named Task Force Red Tango and undertook a successful early-morning parachute assault against Omar Torrijos international airport and Tocumen military airfield to the east of Panama City, thereby permitting the landing of the 82nd Airborne Division, for the loss of one killed, five wounded and 19 jump injuries.

Known as Task Force Red Romeo, the 2nd Battalion and bulk of the 3rd, along with headquarters detachment Team Black, conducted a low-level jump on the airfield at Rio Hato 55 miles (88 km) west of Panama City at 0003 hours and had secured the target within two hours for the loss of four killed, 27 wounded, and 35 parachute injuries. The Rangers then moved out to capture Noriega's nearby beach house.

The various battalions remained in Panama for the next few weeks. They conducted various security missions, hunted down remnants of Panama's regular and paramilitary forces, and secured key positions. By the time of their withdrawal in the second week of January, they had captured over 1,000 enemy personnel and confiscated around 18,000 arms of all types.

The Rangers were next deployed on active service to the Middle East after Saddam Hussein launched Iraqi forces into neighbouring Kuwait in 1990. However, the Ranger presence was small, with only Company B and Company A's 1st Platoon of the 1st Battalion being involved in Operation Desert Storm. The Rangers were deployed in Saudi Arabia from February 12 to April 15, 1991, and undertook hit-and-run raids, reconnaissance patrols, and served as a rapid-reaction force. The liberation of Kuwait was swift and achieved with few casualties among the Coalition forces; the Rangers themselves recorded no losses.

If Desert Storm had been relatively bloodless, the Rangers' next mission was a much bloodier affair. Between August 26 and October 21, 1993, the 3rd Battalion's Company B and a command detachment was despatched to Somalia in the Horn of Africa as part of Operation Restore Hope, a US-led but multinational peace-keeping and humanitarian mission to bring order to a country torn apart by fighting between rival warlords. Task Force Ranger was ordered to capture the most powerful warlord, General Mohammed Farah Aidid, and conducted several sweeps through Mogadishu, the country's capital, in search of its quarry. On October 3 the Rangers raided Mogadishu's Olympic Hotel and then went to the assistance of a Black Hawk helicopter that had been brought down by the warlord's militia. The Rangers were quickly surrounded by thousands of Somalis and, as these were being kept at bay, some of the Rangers attempted to reach the crew of a second Black Hawk that had crashed. All of the Rangers that went to the aid of the second helicopter were killed and two, Master Sergeant Gary Gordon and Sergeant First Class Randall Shughart, were subsequently awarded the Congressional Medal of Honor. The surviving men were eventually evacuated the following day, thanks to the work of other Rangers and a battalion of the US 10th Mountain Division supported by Malayan and Pakistani forces. The intense fighting cost the Rangers 16 killed and 57 wounded.

THE WAR ON TERROR

The terrorist attack on New York's Twin Towers on September 11, 2001, led President George Bush Jr to authorize Operation Enduring Freedom – a worldwide campaign against Osama bin Laden and members of his Al-Qaeda network that had been identified as the perpetrators. Al-Qaeda's chief supporter was the fundamentalist Muslim Taliban regime in Afghanistan and the Rangers were deployed to the country to seek out the terrorists and, along with other Special Forces, aid the anti-government Northern Alliance in toppling the Taliban. The first Ranger action began late on October 19, when 100 Rangers air assaulted a suspected Al-Qaeda compound outside Kandahar and a small airfield in the south of the country. The Rangers successfully seized valuable documents and destroyed several weapons' caches, but two, Specialist Jonn Edmunds and Private First Class Kristofer Stonesifer, died when their helicopter crashed in neighbouring Pakistan.

Over the following months, as the Taliban regime collapsed, the Rangers began to sweep Afghanistan's extensive highlands in search of Bin Laden and Al-Qaeda suspects. Numerous caves were searched and weapons and intelligence on the organization uncovered but the terrorist leader remained at large. In one such operation during May 2002 the Rangers were called upon to respond to an Al-Qaeda group that had ambushed US Navy Seals being helicoptered to a mountain known as Takur Ghar. A 23-man Ranger quick-reaction force based at Gardez went to the Seals' aid but one of their two helicopters was shot down on the upper slopes. The men in the second landed lower down and then climbed the mountain to reach their comrades who were faced by a numerous enemy that was being held off by their fire and close-air support. The two groups were eventually reunited and evacuated under cover of darkness after killing several Al-Qaeda fighters.

The eventual removal of the Taliban and disruption of the terrorist network did not end the war on terror. Osama bin Laden escaped and the worldwide hunt for him continues at the time of writing as does the United States' intention to crush regimes that sponsor terrorism. It seems likely that the Rangers will again be called into action, thereby fulfilling their creed.

Below: In Iraq and Afghanistan, Rangers were involved in a variety of missions, the details of which are still sketchy. The modern Ranger unit is the 75th Regiment, whose shoulder flash mirrors that of the wartime battalions.

ASSESSMENT

The variety of roles undertaken by the Rangers during World War II in part reflected an age-old problem with special forces – what are they for? Most commanders of the time were trained to operate with conventionally organized and equipped brigades, divisions and corps-sized units, not with battalions of specialist infantry numbering a few hundred men. This problem led directly to the diverse multitude of front-line combat missions that the Rangers undertook between 1942 and 1945, and sometimes left them being deployed as nothing more than headquarters security details – a somewhat bizarre job for specialist infantry. This was temporarily the case in northwest Europe in late 1944 and on Luzon in 1945. Although the battalions underwent amphibious assault training and all took part in such operations, the Rangers were deployed on numerous other tasks, only a few of which involved the type of 'ranging' familiar to their eighteenth century counterparts. This very flexibility made the Rangers a prized asset for many senior commanders but for the Rangers themselves it sometimes meant learning on the job. Darby, for example, insisted that his 1st Battalion conduct night-time training during the North African campaign, a decision that was of immense and immediate value.

The Rangers' greatest successes in World War II were chiefly as spearhead assault troops during the opening phase of an amphibious landing. In North Africa, Sicily, at Salerno, Anzio, on D-Day and at Leyte Gulf they conducted operations, most involving neutralizing coastal defences, designed to ease the way for the main assault forces. Despite the dangers associated with such missions, most were quickly completed and, with the exception of the Pointe du Hoc assault on D-Day, achieved at little cost due to the speed of the Rangers' attacks and the often low-grade opposition they faced. Pointe du Hoc was an altogether tougher proposition as all of the other landings were conducted across nothing more than gently shelving beaches or low sea-walls and, by attacking under cover of darkness or at early dawn, the Rangers enjoyed an element of surprise. On D-Day, the Rangers had none of these factors in their favour yet they persevered and successfully stormed the cliff-top position. Despite their heavy losses the assault was undoubtedly one of the finest moments of June 6 and its inherent dangers were recognized by General Omar Bradley. In his autobiography, he remarked in reference to Lieutenant Colonel James Rudder, commander of the assault companies: 'No soldier in my command has ever been wished a more difficult task than that which befell the 34-year-old commander of this Provisional Ranger Force.'

Yet the Rangers were also called upon to conduct other missions and here the results were more mixed. There was mountain fighting in Tunisia, Sicily and Italy, attacks against fixed defences in northwest Europe after D-Day, and in an echo of the past, patrols and reconnaissance missions similar to those pioneered by the Ranger companies of colonial America. The results of the mountain fighting were generally favourable if occasionally costly. The Rangers were successful in Tunisia, Sicily, at Salerno and around Cassino,

BATTLE HONOURS FLAG

To celebrate the outstanding contribution of the Ranger battalions during World War II, the US Army Heraldic Branch designed a commemorative flag to reflect their history and combat record. It consists of a rectangular flag divided in two diagonally from top left to bottom right. The upper, darker half symbolizes the United States, while the lower scarlet portion represents Great Britain, where many of the units were trained and based. In the centre a white circle is used to represent Central Europe, chiefly Germany, while a superimposed black fleur-de-lys represents service in France and the Low Countries. Similarly red seed pods allude to service in Italy, while a double crescent indicates the campaigns in Algeria and Tunisia. Three sun rays indicate the role of the 6th Battalion in the Philippines, while crossed knives, based on the British Fairbairn-Sykes design for the Commandos, indicate the types of operation undertaken by the Rangers.

although the perils involved in fighting at altitude in winter were reflected in the high casualty suffered by the battalions in the last case. Attacking fixed defences is not usually considered the role of specialist light infantry, yet the Rangers were undoubtedly a valuable asset in capturing Brest during the late summer of 1944.

With regard to patrols, raids and larger operations involving movement through and behind enemy lines, during World War II the Rangers achieved some of their greatest successes – and one of their greatest defeats – in this way. Sened in Tunisia was an early indication of their capabilities and was followed by two highly regarded operations, at Irsch–Zerf in February 1945 and the Cabanatuan raid in January 1945. Both earned the units involved a Presidential Unit Citation, and the latter, which was the subject of a photo essay in *Life* by renowned war photographer Carl Mydans, brought the 6th Battalion immense fame in the United States. So intense was the media interest, the battalion's after-action report concluded that, 'If it lasted one more day, more buttons would have to be sewn on and larger hat sizes secured. The men were walking on air.' Yet Irsch–Zerf and Cabanatuan have to be balanced by the disaster at Anzio. Operation Shingle was badly managed for the most part but the the effective loss of three battalions outside Cisterna in January 1944 was one of its lowest points and an acute embarrassment to the Allies. Little blame can be attached to the battalions involved and the defeat did not end the Rangers' contribution to the Allied victory as a further three battalions took their place.

Above: Rangers saw action in both European and Pacific theatres. This is Company F of 6th Rangers patrolling on Dinagat Island.

The Rangers chief weakness was that they were essentially light infantry trained for swift and short-lived operations, not prolonged fighting. For the most part the standard battalions were equipped with nothing more powerful than light/medium mortars and machine guns. Such weapons were suitable for fast-moving operations against light opposition that were expected to last only a few hours but proved inadequate against stronger opposition. Action reports also frequently speak of shortages of ammunition – a situation that reflected the Rangers' lack of integral logistical support. Indeed, it was not uncommon for Rangers to seek out other units for such supplies and they constantly had to rely on external mechanized transport. There were attempts to beef up their firepower by adding, for example, the Cannon Company, or seconding units with heavier weapons to them, but the battalions continued to rely on outside support, whether from warships or other independent ground units. During the final stages of the war in Europe, the situation was largely reversed. The Rangers were starved of opportunities to act independently and units were no longer being attached to them, rather it was the Rangers themselves that were being attached. Nevertheless the Rangers had an outstanding combat record and few units of a comparable size matched the range and number of hazardous mission they successfully completed before their temporary demise at the end of the conflict.

REFERENCE

INTERNET SITES

http://www.ranger.org
A site produced by the US Army Ranger Association containing pages on operations, honours, unit histories and related links. It also offers Ranger-related material for sale.

http://www.ranger.org/usara/s5/assoc/darby/darbys.htm
Home of the Darby Foundation, which is based at Fort Smith, Arizona, and is dedicated to preserving the memory of the founder of the World War II Rangers.

http://www.rangermemorial.org
The home page of the Ranger Memorial Foundation, an organization that created and maintains the Ranger memorial at Fort Benning, Georgia; the site also includes details of Ranger-related events.

http://www.ranger.org/usara/s3/Ops/wwii/wwii.htm
The site run by the Ranger Battalions Association of World War II recounts the history of the Rangers from colonial America to the present but concentrates on their exploits in World War II. It also provides information on the modern Ranger Training Brigade, unit honours and Congressional Medal of Honor winners.

http://www.ricakw.org
The Association of Ranger Infantry Companies of the Korean War, a body dedicated to recounting the story of those who served during the conflict.

http://www.75thrra.org/
An association for members of the 75th Ranger Regiment and associated units, mostly from the Vietnam War, with pages detailing forthcoming events.

http://www.grunts.net/army/rangers.html
The history of the Rangers from colonial America to the present, which also contains some Medal of Honor citations and links to other sites.

http://www2.gdi.net/agengreb
The Brotherhood of Rangers home page that includes pages on the Ranger Creed and links to additional sites.

http://www-cgsc.army.mil/carl/resources/csi/King/King.asp#B1
Part of the Command & General Staff College's Combined Arms Research Library

resources, this consists of Leavenworth Papers No. 11 by Dr. Michael J. King, which is an exhaustive account of several Ranger operations in World War II including those at Djebel el Ank, Porto Empedocle, Cisterna, Zerf and Cabanatuan. Also includes useful bibliography.

http://www.goarmy.com/job/branch/sorc/75th/Rangers.htm
A site from the US Army providing information for prospective Ranger candidates. It also has pages on their modern role, training and background history.

http://www.specialoperations.com/Army/Rangers/default2.html
Provides information on the Ranger School and training course as well as a profile of the modern unit and its antecedents.

http://suasponte.com/index/.html
Details of the Rangers' history, their creed and a quiz.

http:www.2ndRangers.org/
A St. Louis, Missouri, group of World War II re-enactors.

BIBLIOGRAPHY

Altieri, James J.: *Darby's Rangers: An Illustrated Portrayal of the Original Rangers.* The Seeman Printery, 1945.
A history of the 1st, 3rd and 4th Rangers by one who served with them. The book is illustrated and written by a past president of the Ranger Association.

Bahmanyar, Mir, and Welply, Michael: *US Army Ranger, 1983–2001 – Sua Sponte: Of Their Own Accord.* Osprey, 2003
A highly illustrated account of the modern Rangers, their campaigns, battles, equipment and training.

Breuer, William B.: *The Great Raid on Cabanatuan – Rescuing the Doomed Ghosts of Bataan and Corregidor.* John Wiley and Sons, 1994.
A history of the famed rescue of US prisoners on Luzon during World War II and the basis for a forthcoming film.

Darby, William O., and Baumer, William H.: *Darby's Rangers – We Led the Way.* Presidio Press, 1990.
Based on conversations between Darby and Baumer in 1944, this recounts the formation of the Rangers, their training and operations from Dieppe to Italy involving the 1st, 3rd and 4th Battalions. It also includes brief summaries of missions conducted by the 2nd and 5th Battalions in northwest Europe and the 6th Battalion in the Philippines.

Drez, Ronald J.: *Voices of D-Day – The Story of the Allied Invasion Told by Those Who Were There.* Louisiana State University Press, 1994.
Contains a chapter that has first-hand accounts from survivors of the 2nd and 5th Ranger Battalions who assaulted the Pointe du Hoc cliffs and landed on Omaha Beach on June 6, 1944.

Eshel, David: *Daring to Win – Special Forces at War.* Arms and Armour Press, 1992.
Recounts action by various special forces on land, at sea and in the air from World War I to

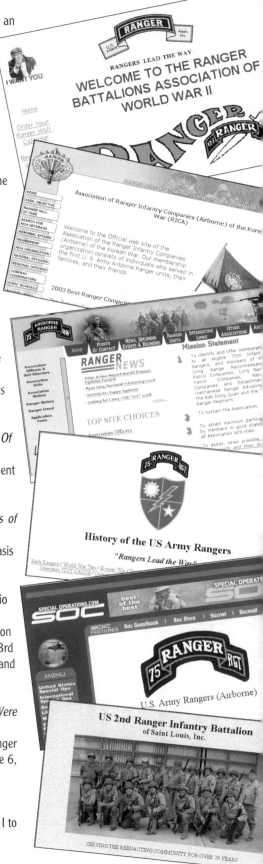

Operation Desert Storm. One chapter deals with the Rangers' assault on the Pointe du Hoc on D-Day and another is on their role during the 1983 invasion of Grenada.

Field, Ron: *Ranger – Behind Enemy Lines in Vietnam*. Publishing News, 2000.
The core of the book concentrates on Ranger-style units of the Vietnam War, but also includes sections on the early history of such units from colonial America to the Indian Wars of the second half of the nineteenth century. A final section looks at modern Ranger campaigns from Operation Eagle Claw in 1980 to Operation Restore Hope in the early 1990s.

Garrett, Richard: *The Raiders*. David & Charles, 1980.
A study of special forces' operations through the ages that contains a chapter on the capture of the Pointe du Hoc on D-Day.

Johnson, Forrest Bryant: *Hour of Redemption: The Ranger Raid on Cabanatuan*. Manor Books, 1978.
The story of the daring behind-the-lines mission spearheaded by elements of the 6th Rangers to rescue US prisoners of war in 1945.

Krueger, Walter: *From Down Under to Nippon – The Story of the Sixth Army in World War II*. Combat Forces Press, 1953.
The commander of the US Sixth Army and the driving force behind the creation of the 6th Rangers recounts his part in the Pacific campaign.

King, Michael J.: *William Orlando Darby – A Military Biography*. Archon Books, 1981.
A review of the life and military career of the founder of the Rangers during World War II by an officer who attended the US Army Airborne and Ranger Schools.

Lane, Ronald L.: *Rudder's Rangers: The True Story of the 2nd Ranger Battalion D-Day Combat Action*. Ranger Association, 1995.
A history of the 2nd Ranger Battalion and its operation to storm the Pointe du Hoc on D-Day.

Lanning, Michael Lee, *Inside the LRRPs: Rangers in Vietnam*. Ivy Books, 1988.
The story of the revival of the Ranger concept and their role during the Southeast Asia conflict.

Lucas, James: *Commandos and Rangers of World War II*. Macdonald and Jane's, 1978.
A review of British and US Commando-type units that covers Ranger operations during the war and has useful information on weapons and equipment.

McDonald, Joanna M.: *The Liberation of the Pointe du Hoc: the 2d Rangers at Normandy, June 6–8, 1944*. Rank and File Publications, 2000.
An account of one of the epic actions of the Normandy landings, including the origins of the battalion and a facsimile of the Presidential Unit Citation it was awarded.

Macksey, Kenneth: *Commando Strike – The Story of Amphibious Raiding in World War II*. Leo Cooper and Secker & Warburg, 1985.
Although concentrating on British operations, this overview provides a useful introduction to the development of US special forces, including Rangers, during the conflict and covers some of their actions.

O'Donnell, Patrick K.: *Beyond Valor – World War II's Ranger and Airborne Veterans Reveal the Heat of Combat.* Touchstone Books, 2002.
Hundreds of first-hand accounts of Rangers and airborne personnel detailing their experiences from North Africa to the final battles in Europe.

Prince, Morris: *The Story of the Elite WWII 2nd Battalion Rangers.* Meadowlark Publishing, 2001.
A first-hand account by a private in the battalion's Company A following the unit's actions from D-Day to VE-Day.

Rottman, Gordon L., and Volstad, Ron: *US Army Rangers & LRRP Units, 1942–87.* Osprey, 1987
An outline history of the Rangers and associated units from World War II to the invasion of Grenada.

Rottman, Gordon, and Volstad, Ron: *Panama, 1989–90.* Osprey Publishing, 1991
An overview of the US invasion and occupation of the Central American dictatorship including details of the participation of the Rangers.

Sides, Hampton: *Ghost Soldiers – The Astonishing Story of One of Wartime's Greatest Escapes.* Time Warner, 2002.
An exhaustive but highly readable account of the mission by the 6th Ranger Battalion to release Japanese-held prisoners at Cabanatuan on Luzon during early 1945.

Truscott, Lucian K., Jr., *Command Missions: A Personal Story.* New York, 1954.
The excellent autobiographical account of one of the US Army's most skilled battlefield commanders and the officer most responsible for the formation of the Rangers in World War II.

MEMORIALS

The most evocative and moving memorial to the exploits of the Rangers in World War II is situated atop the Pointe du Hoc in Normandy. Lying some 8 miles (13 km) west of the US cemetery overlooking Omaha Beach, it consists of a single granite pylon positioned on the remains of a German concrete bunker and at its feet are tablets inscribed in English and French. Originally erected by the French to honour the operation, it was formally transferred to the care of the American Battle Monuments Commission in January 1979.

A second site associated with the Rangers is also cared for by the commission. This is the Cabanatuan American Memorial on Luzon, which lies on the site of the former prisoner of war camp and honours those Americans and Filipinos who died during their captivity. It was erected by survivors of the Bataan Death March and former prisoners of Cabanatuan.

In the United States, there is a monument at Fort Benning, Georgia, located in front of the Infantry School outside Building 4. It was erected by the Ranger Memorial Foundation in 1994 and was mostly funded by ex-Rangers and their families. Its chief features are the memorial stones that record the names and units of former Rangers, but not their ranks.

In Northern Ireland there is an exhibition based around the early history of the Rangers during World War II. Located in the grounds of the Andrew Jackson Centre at Boneybefore, Carrickfergus, is the US Rangers Centre. There is also a memorial stone at nearby Sunnylands Camp where the first recruits were billeted.

FILMS

The exploits of the Rangers have been a popular source of material for Hollywood over the years. One of the earliest movies to be released on the subject starred Spencer Tracy as Robert Rogers. Directed by King Vidor and released in 1940, *Northwest Passage* is based on a 1937 novel by Kenneth Roberts and recounts the 1759 raid on the Abenaki at St. Francis. The running time is 126 minutes and the supporting cast included Robert Young and Walter Brennan. William Wellman directed *Darby's Rangers* in 1958 and this 122-minute movie stars James Garner as Darby and covers the raising of the unit and its combat service. More recently Ridley Scott was inspired by the Ranger operation in Somalia to film *Blackhawk Down*, which was released in 2002. With a running time of 144 minutes, it was inspired by a book by Mark Bowden and stars Josh Hartnett and Ewan McGregor. Finally, there is a projected film of the 6th Battalion's Cabanatuan mission in the pipeline. Directed by John Dahl, *The Great Raid* stars Benjamin Bratt and Joseph Fiennes and filming began in Queensland, Australia, in early July 2002. A 2003 release date is expected.

INDEX